Gilles Paquet

Tackling Wicked Policy Problems

Equality, Diversity and Sustainability

Collaborative Decentred Metagovernance Series

This series of books is designed to define cumulatively the contours of collaborative decentred metagovernance. At this time, there is still no canonical version of this paradigm: it is *en émergence*. This series intends to be one of many 'construction sites' to experiment with various dimensions of an effective and practical version of this new approach.

Metagovernance is the art of combining different forms or styles of governance, experimented with in the private, public and social sectors, to ensure effective coordination when power, resources and information are widely distributed, and the governing is of necessity decentred and collaborative.

The series invites conceptual and practical contributions focused on different issue domains, policy fields, *causes célèbres*, functional processes, etc. to the extent that they contribute to sharpening the new apparatus associated with collaborative decentred metagovernance.

In the last few decades, there has been a need felt for a more sophisticated understanding of the governing of the private, public and social sectors: for less compartmentalization among sectors that have much in common; and for new conceptual tools to suggest new relevant questions and new ways to carry out the business of governing, by creatively recombining the tools of governance that have proved successful in all these sectors. These efforts have generated experiments that have been sufficiently rich and wide-ranging in the various laboratories to warrant efforts to pull together what we know at this stage.

This fourth book in the series attempts to contribute somewhat to accelerating the process of recognition of governance studies as a heuristically powerful field of study, by providing some building blocks likely to be of help in the construction of a much needed synthetic framework. It does so in two distinct ways: first, through a report on the evolution of governance studies; and, second, through some experiments using the governance approach to tackle some wicked trans-scientific policy challenges – equality, diversity and sustainability.

Interested parties are invited to join the Chautauqua.

– Editorial Board

Other titles published by INVENIRE are listed at the end of this book.

Gilles Paquet

Tackling Wicked Policy Problems

Equality, Diversity and Sustainability

Collaborative Decentred Metagovernance Series
INVENIRE BOOKS

Ottawa, Canada
2013

University of Ottawa **Press**
Les **Presses** de l'Université d'Ottawa

The University of Ottawa Press (UOP) is proud to be the oldest of the francophone university presses in Canada and the oldest bilingual university publisher in North America. Since 1936, UOP has been enriching intellectual and cultural discourse by producing peer-reviewed and award-winning books in the humanities and social sciences, in French and in English.

www.Press.uOttawa.ca

Library and Archives Canada Cataloguing in Publication

Title: Tackling wicked policy problems : equality, diversity and sustainability / Gilles Paquet.
Names: Paquet, Gilles, author.
Series: Collaborative decentred metagovernance series ; v. 4.
Description: Series statement: Collaborative decentred metagovernance series ; v. 4 | Reprint.
        Originally published: Ottawa, Canada : Invenire Books, 2013. | Includes bibliographical references.
Identifiers: Canadiana (print) 20220286426 | Canadiana (ebook) 20220286442 | ISBN 9780776638645 (softcover) | ISBN 9780776638652 (PDF) | ISBN 9780776638669 (EPUB)
Subjects: LCSH: Public administration. | LCSH: Political science. | LCSH: Management. | LCSH: Social policy.
Classification: LCC JF1351 .P275 2022 | DDC 351—dc23

This book was initially published by Invenire Books in 2013 in the Collaborative Decentered Metagovernance Series. The cover design, layout and design were produced by Sandy Lynch. The University of Ottawa Press reissued this book thanks to the support of Ontario Creates.

Invenire

Invenire Books, an Ottawa-based idea factory that operated from 2010 to 2019, specialized in collaborative governance and stewardship. Invenire and its authors provide creative practical and stimulating responses to the challenges and opportunities faced by today's organizations. The list is now carried by the University of Ottawa Press.

Profession: Public Servant
The Entrepreneurial Effect: Practical Ideas from Your Own Virtual Board of Advisors
La flotte blanche : histoire de la compagnie de navigation du Richelieu et d'Ontario
Tableau d'avancement II : essais exploratoires sur la gouvernance d'un certain Canada français
The Entrepreneurial Effect: Waterloo
The Unimagined Canadian Capital: Challenges for the Federal Capital Region
The State in Transition: Challenges for Canadian Federalism
Cities as Crucibles: Reflections on Canada's Urban Future
Gouvernance communautaire : innovations dans le Canada français hors Québec
Through the Detox Prism: Exploring Organizational Failures and Design Responses
Cities and Languages: Governance and Policy – An International Symposium
Villes et langues : gouvernance et politiques – symposium international
Moderato Cantabile: Toward Principled Governance for Canada's Immigration Policy
Stewardship: Collaborative Decentred Metagovernance and Inquiring Systems
Challenges in Public Health Governance: The Canadian Experience
Innovation in Canada: Why We Need More and What We Must Do to Get It
Challenges of Minority Governments in Canada
Gouvernance corporative : une entrée en matières

Tackling Wicked Policy Problems: Equality, Diversity and Sustainability
50 ans de bilinguisme officiel : défis, analyses et témoignages
Unusual Suspects: Essays on Social Learning
Probing the Bureaucratic Mind: About Canadian Federal Executives
Tableau d'avancement III : pour une diaspora canadienne-française antifragile
Autour de Chantal Mouffe : le politique en conflit
Town and Crown: An Illustrated History of Canada's Capital
The Tainted-Blood Tragedy in Canada: A Cascade of Governance Failures
Intelligent Governance: A Prototype for Social Coordination
Driving the Fake Out of Public Administration: Detoxing HR in the Canadian Federal Public Sector
Tableau d'avancement IV : un Canada français à ré-inventer
A Future for Economics: More Encompassing, More Institutional, More Practical
Pasquinade in F : essais à rebrousse-poil
Building Bridges: Case Studies in Collaborative Governance in Canada
Scheming Virtuously: The Road to Collaborative Governance
A Lantern on the Bow: A History of the Science Council of Canada and its Contributions to the Science and Innovation Policy Debate
Fifty Years of Official Bilingualism: Challenges, Analyses and Testimonies
Irregular Governance: A Plea for Bold Organizational Experimentation
Pasquinade in E: Slaughtering Some Sacred Cows

The University of Ottawa Press gratefully acknowledges the support extended to its publishing list by the Government of Canada, the Canada Council for the Arts, the Ontario Arts Council, the Social Sciences and Humanities Research Council and the Canadian Federation for the Humanities and Social Sciences through the Awards to Scholarly Publications Program, and by the University of Ottawa.

ONTARIO ARTS COUNCIL
CONSEIL DES ARTS DE L'ONTARIO
an Ontario government agency
un organisme du gouvernement de l'Ontario

Canada Council   Conseil des arts
for the Arts   du Canada

Canada

uOttawa

"I propose the term *trans-scientific* for these questions since, though they are, epistemologically speaking, questions of fact and can be stated in the language of science, they are unanswerable by science; they transcend science."

– *Alvin M. Weinberg*

Table of Contents

TABLES AND FIGURES

| Introduction

The literature in governance studies has been scattered in very many directions over the last 25 years. This is the fate of any issue domain where the literature is fueled by an emerging paradigm. There is, as yet, no canon in governance studies, so any newcomer to this literature is likely to be bamboozled by the variety of competing definitions in use for key terms, the many conceptual frameworks experimented with, and the excessive statements by friends and foes of the approach to its promises and its limitations.

The ebullition of this governance studies literature over the last quarter of a century, and the number of controversies it has generated, have been such that no one has yet chronicled its evolution in an effective, reasoned, and comprehensive way. Such a synthetic work would appear to be still beyond reach for the moment.

On the one hand at the governance-management frontier, the squabbling of financial accountants and lawyers to defend their hegemony on the governance territory has generated an immense amount of noise about the plumbing aspects of governance, but not much light on the governance *problematique*. These professions, focused almost exclusively on financial reporting and on the etiquette of board management, still pretend that their very limiting perspectives fully exhaust the substance of governing. As a result, they have whimsically claimed that since they have tilled that territory, there is nothing left of substance for lay governance experts to uncover.

On the other hand at the broader front of organization science – a very diffuse nebula that is also trying to establish its turf and credibility – governance studies are regarded as a rather narrow, specialized field pertaining to the stewardship of organizations. It may have some exotic interests, but does not appear to hold the promise of any epistemological revolutionary breakthrough.

Yet, despite the fact that it is not well recognized, the multiplication of experiments in governance studies has already accomplished much. While it may not yet have gelled into a formalized and stylized field of study, officially recognized in many quarters crippled by corporate or ideological traditions, it brings forth an original perspective, a different *manière de voir*, an enlightening analytical framework, a promising language of problem definition, and a most useful clinical apparatus and mental tool box to track down the sources and causes of organizational dysfunction, and develop and design repairs to ensure effective stewardship.

This short book attempts to contribute somewhat to accelerating the process of recognition of governance studies as a heuristically powerful field of study, by providing some building blocks likely to be of help in the construction of a much needed synthetic framework. It does so in two distinct ways: first, through a report on the evolution of governance studies; and, second, through some experiments using the governance approach to tackle some trans-scientific policy challenges – equality, diversity and sustainability.

Part I provides snapshots of the state of play in governance studies.

Chapter 1 focuses on the most dramatic transformation in the organizational landscape over the last half century – the drift from Big 'G' (government) to small 'g' (governance) in the public, private and social sectors. Governance is presented as providing a third way between the two dominant cosmologies that have been in good currency over the last century – type-I liberalism and its focus on freedom and decentralization, and type-II liberalism and its focus on statism and centralization. The many oscillations between these two poles are explored, as well as the different waves in the evolution of the notion of governance. New developments are hinted at.

Chapter 2 takes a first stab at defining the contours of the governance *problematique*, and the transformations it suggests to the conceptual frameworks in good currency. Then it hints at the sort of difficulties governance has met in establishing its legitimacy as a promising third-way *vis-à-vis* the two *problematiques* in good currency. Finally, it reflects in a preliminary way on both the promises and the limitations of governance studies.

Chapter 3 explores the epistemological drift that has proved necessary for governance studies to emerge as an effective approach to tackling wicked policy problems. Wicked problems are those where ends are unknown or not agreed upon, and means-ends relationships are either poorly understood or not stable. Given their complexity, and the focus on an effort *to create a wholly new unprecedented situation,* many of the wicked policy problems facing governance studies "are unanswerable by science; they transcend science."[1] Studies of such problems are of necessity somewhat imprecise because they inhabit the republic of trans-science – bordering on both the political, social, economic, cultural and moral republics, and the republic of science.[2]

Chapter 3 is quite ambitious. It provides a broad-brushed picture of the social learning approach developed at the Centre

---

[1] The focus is not on attempts to falsify hypotheses about some objective reality. We are faced with a context where entities are defined by their environment and their relationships with others, where one wishes to create new knowledge and design systems that do not exist yet – not establishing the truth-value of propositions about an object reality in abstraction from the context (John Friedmann and George Abonyi. 1976. "Social Learning: A Model for Policy Research," *Environment and Planning A*, (8): 927-940). This subject matter is too volatile, and the concepts are too contested for scientific canons to apply. It involves the public, and the legitimate viewpoints are too many, so moral and political judgment may prevail. In the republic of trans-science, it is not the wisdom of the expert that dominates or should dominate because experts have only a portion of the relevant knowledge (Alvin M. Weinberg. 1974. "Science and Trans-science," *Minerva*, 10(2): 209-222).

[2] Gilles Paquet. 1999. "Tackling Wicked Problems" in G. Paquet. *Governance Through Social Learning*. Ottawa, ON: The University of Ottawa Press, chapter 2; Gilles Paquet. 2012. "La gouvernance, science de l'imprécis," *Organisations & Territoires*, 21(3): 5-17.

on Governance of the University of Ottawa over the last 15 years: the basic questions at the origin of the inquiry, the assumptions on which the inquiry is based, the four major components of the engine of social learning and 'wayfinding', the new focus on design thinking, on the development of a design attitude, and on the way in which such an attitude based on mindfulness can be engineered. Much of this picture is only elliptically sketched, but it provides a summary view of the approach used in Part II.

In Part II, the book tackles three wicked trans-scientific policy questions: equality, diversity and sustainability.

These three questions are rooted in contested concepts that connote and convey a wide range of meanings for different individuals and groups. They have generated a following for these diverse interpretations, and have spawned ideologically-charged debates. Moreover, they pose empirical (socio-economic and political) but additionally epistemic, cultural and moral problems.

Chapter 4 tackles the debate around equality. The question of equality has become not only a ruling ideology, but a seemingly unchallengeable reference point in democratic societies. This chapter shows that the notion of equality is a contested concept, and it has been interpreted and misinterpreted in a great variety of ways. Indeed, it has been a rather toxic driver in democratic society. As Tocqueville persuasively argued, "democratic peoples ... have an ardent, insatiable, eternal, invincible passion for equality; they want equality in liberty, and, if they cannot obtain it, they want it in slavery."[3] Moreover, as Tocqueville also observed, "the desire for equality becomes ever more insatiable as equality increases."[4] Indeed, the dogma of egalitarianism – a radical version of the search for equality – has been shown to foster tension, envy and violence.[5] The challenge is to sketch the

[3] Alexis de Tocqueville. 1961 [1840]. *De la démocratie en Amérique*. Paris, FR: Gallimard, vol. 2, p. 104.

[4] *Ibid.*, p. 144.

[5] Paul Laurent and Gilles Paquet. 1991. "Intercultural Relations: A Myrdal-Tocqueville-Girard Interpretation Scheme," *International Political Science Review*, 13(3): 173-185.

contours of a meaningful governance of equability (acceptable inequality) as a preferred option.

Chapter 5 deals with the challenge of diversity: the challenge generated by the great shuffling of population that has led to the commingling of deeply different cultural groups in the last century, and to significant and often deadly inter-group conflicts around matters of identity.[6]

In the case of Canada, the whole diversity issue has been made even more agonistic by the compounding of this population shuffle with a nexus of policies (immigration, multiculturalism) that would appear to be defined on the basis of the ideology that the optimum of diversity is the maximum of diversity. A crucial challenge is to elicit a meaningful governance of diversity that takes into account the fragile social fabric of our democratic societies.[7]

Chapter 6 raises the complex discussion of sustainability. It identifies some of the obstacles that prevent social scientists from answering the basic question, "what should we try to sustain?" Moreover, it shows that what is required is a mental tool box capable of blending the different dimensions of sustainability into a syncretic perspective, and it puts forward modest general propositions for a family of mechanisms likely to ensure a workable governance regime.

The governance of equality, diversity and sustainability will be probed, in turn, with a view to designing wayfinding systems likely to generate the sort of stewardship capable of generating resilience and innovation on a scale commensurate with the criticality of the challenges these questions raise. This will be done by engineering some reconciliation of the diverse frames of reference, and some effective collaboration of all those who have a significant portion of power, resources and information in these issue domains.

The responses to these challenges transcend science. Yet social scientists, mesmerized by decades of positivistic

---

[6] Amin Maalouf. 2001. *Les identités meurtrières*. Paris, FR: Livre de Poche.

[7] Raymond Breton et al. 2004. *A Fragile Social Fabric? Fairness, Trust and Commitment in Canada*. Montreal, QC and Kingston, ON: McGill-Queen's University Press.

preaching, often refuse to recognize the limitations of their traditional approaches. They are often in denial about where science ends and where trans-science begins, and display much ingenuity in the use of devices to forcefully deport their research questions from their natural habitat in the republic of trans-science to an artificial scientific turf. Unreasonable assumptions and ideological reductionism underpin such shifty operations.

So governance studies have to deal not only with the hyper-complexity of the issue domains of interest, and with the multiplicity of legitimate perspectives on these questions, but they also have to defend their analyses and results against the defamation of dreadful simplifiers who argue their case on the basis of amazingly contorted 'scientistic cartoons' originating from the catatonia of crippling mental prisons.

The conclusion of this volume conjectures on the possible futures to be expected from governance studies at some important frontiers.

I would like to acknowledge the professional help of the Invenire Books team (McEvoy Galbreath, Anne Phillips and Sandy Lynch) for seeing the manuscript through the publication process with great skill.

The support of the Centre on Governance at the University of Ottawa is gratefully acknowledged.

PART I
State of Play

The three chapters of Part I take the reader into a funnel.

Chapter 1 provides a broad picture of the two main contrasting perspectives on governing that have been in good currency in the last century (type-I liberalism and type-II liberalism) and shows how the notion of governance has emerged as a third option in response to the limitations of the first two in resolving the coordination problem.

Chapter 2 sketches a stylized version of the governance approach, shows how it transforms key concepts in use, questions the persiflage about this approach by various groups most reluctant to reframe their view of the world, and offers some conjectures about the future of governance studies and the central role of design thinking within it.

Chapter 3 presents the most recent version of the evolving social learning approach developed at the Centre on Governance of the University of Ottawa to tackle wicked policy problems. It sketches the questions that have led the inquiry in this general direction, the contours of the four components of the social learning approach, and the reasons why the design attitude is so important in this sort of work – specifically, what it entails, and how to proceed to engineer the sort of inquiring system designed for transience and incompleteness that allow emergent structures to develop.

| Slouching Toward a Relatively Stateless State

*"... 'the stateless state' in which patterns of rules are
the contingent products of diverse actions and political
struggles informed by the beliefs rooted in traditions ..."*

R.A.W. Rhodes

Introduction

Over the last 60 years, two major economic paradigms have struggled to impose their hegemony on the Western world: the views of Friedrich Hayek and Milton Friedman on the one hand, and the views of John Maynard Keynes and John Kenneth Galbraith on the other. In both cases, these pairs of names connote less a unified doctrine than a cosmology and a range of beliefs that may be broadly associated with type-I liberalism and type-II liberalism for lack of better labels for these nebulae.[1]

My purpose is neither to propose a facile comparison that would fail to do justice to cosmologies replete with so many subtle and not so subtle differences (even within the same tribe), nor to attempt the impossible task of a comprehensive analysis that would be out of the question in a short chapter.

---

[1] *Stanford Encyclopedia of Philosophy*, "Liberalism," http://plato.stanford.edu/
entries/liberalism/ (revised September 16, 2010), [accessed February 10, 2012].

I will only use these two reference points in the intellectual landscape of the 20th century in order to draw attention to their limitations in providing guidance to handle the central economic question – the problem of coordination[2] – as a result of their overly restrictive focalization on certain instruments: market and competition in the one case, and state and technocracy in the other. This will set the stage for my argument that the emergence of the notion of governance has been an evolving response to the failures of both of these cosmologies in effectively tackling the coordination problem.

The first section sketches the broad contours of the two basic cosmologies, signals their evolving relative importance over time, and draws attention to some key limitations in their dealing with the problem of coordination. The second section introduces a third *manière de voir* (broadly labelled governance) – also a nebula – that has come to occupy a larger place in recent decades and spells out how this new *problematique* has unfolded in three waves. I explain why this represents a genuine alternative to the hyper-focus on market and state in the earlier cosmologies; how it marshals a Quantum outlook quite different from the Newtonian outlook of traditional approaches; and why this third cosmology is more promising as a way to tackle the problem of coordination because it suggests using hybrid arrangements to cope with the baroque situations in our complex world.

Two reference points

The intellectual landscape of the 19th and 20th centuries has been dominated first by type-I liberalism, then by statism (type-II liberalism), and then by a slow movement back toward type-I liberalism. But both families of dominant beliefs, even when they seemed to be out of favour, have continued to exert much influence.

---

[2] Gerald P. O'Driscoll. 1977. *Economics as a Coordination Problem*. Kansas City, MO: Sheed Andrews and McMeel Inc.

The drift back and forth

The spirit of type-I liberalism thrived in the 19ᵗʰ century. It emerged as a reaction to various forms of coercion imposed by tradition and autocratic governing structures that constrained the scope of individual freedom in what was slowly becoming a more open society. This philosophy was not arguing for anarchy, but for reducing coercion to a minimum. So type-I liberalism never entailed (except in its radical fringes) a rejection of state action altogether.

Type-I liberalism *à la* Hayek, for instance, fully recognizes the limited information and knowledge at the disposition of any actor (even the state) at any point in time, and therefore the consequent limitation of human reason in human affairs. This explains why he rejected intrusive state interventionism – condemned as based on much ignorance – and celebrated processes that had the capacity to generate learning, new information and knowledge, and to transmit them (through markets, competition and the like).[3] This was also the message of Milton Friedman, although Friedman remained a positivist (defending the application of experimental science methodologies in the social sciences), while Hayek was arguing forcefully that the methods of the experimental sciences were ill-suited to the study of society.[4]

It is important to repeat that neither Friedman nor Hayek condemned state intervention *per se* (although their opponents have unjustly accused them of doing so), for type-I liberals recognize, for instance, the need for a sound legal framework for the market order to function well, and for the state to be involved when the market fails miserably – as in the case of the provision of public goods. However, the fundamental thrust of type-I liberalism is to limit state intervention as much as possible and, in particular, to limit state monopolies.

---

[3] Friedrich A. Hayek. 1948. *Individualism and Economic Order.* Chicago, IL: The University of Chicago Press.

[4] Friedrich A. Hayek. 1952. *Scientism and the Study of Society.* Glencoe, IL: The Free Press; Milton Friedman. 1953. *Essays in Positive Economics.* Chicago, IL: The University of Chicago Press.

The type-I liberalism cosmology perceives that power, resources and information are broadly distributed among a diversity of actors, that no one (including the state) is fully in charge, and that most institutions and rules are not so much the result of rationally planned human action, but the result of some configuration of various forces generating the emergence of a more or less spontaneous order that often acquires a life of its own. As a result, its crystallized shape may not necessarily resemble any of the templates originally envisaged by any one of the actors. So the emergence and evolution of coordinating arrangements need not necessarily require a masterminding architect in charge. But this does not mean that interested stakeholders cannot try to nudge these processes along through *bricolage*.

Private property is central to this cosmology because it provides individuals with a crucial instrument with which to exercise their freedom. Individuals attempt to maximize their levels of welfare, and their actions lead to inequalities justified by differential aptitudes, competencies and efforts. Inequality within bounds is acceptable to type-I liberals who would in no way support interventions to forcefully ensure the strict equality of outcomes.

While celebrated for its criticism of dictatorship, arbitrary power, intolerance, repression, etc., type-I liberalism has been criticized as unduly naïve in not recognizing that the actions of individuals may be irrational, destructive and stupid, and therefore toxic and capable of inflicting important collective damage. Indeed, such predatory behaviour (whether deliberate or as a result of unintended consequences) had already been observed in earlier times, and led to commissions of inquiry (on child labour, poverty, relations between labour and capital, and the like) that revealed abuse and recommended ways to mitigate the collective harm generated by absolute *laissez-faire*.

The growth of labour unions and state regulations constituted a reaction to coordination failures and collective harm that had resulted from the high-tide of type-I liberalism. The first victim of these correctives was the word 'liberalism' itself – which, over time, was transmogrified and took on a meaning that was the very obverse of its original meaning. What is nowadays called type-II liberalism or statism connotes the idea that freedom is no longer the central concern. What is central in this new view is egalitarianism, and a vision of the state as being charged with the superior burden of office of ensuring the sort of equality of outcomes that has been regarded in recent times as necessary for citizens to be able to exercise their autonomy and freedom. The role of the state is no longer to protect freedom from encroachment (negative liberty), but to provide, as a matter of entitlement, all that is purported to be necessary for citizens to be able to fully exercise their rights to personal development (positive liberty).[5]

Even though the spirit of statism (type-II liberalism) was at first directed to correcting gross market failures and social injustices, over time its ambit has become much more encompassing and intrusive. It has reached the point where type-II liberalism has become a general indictment of type-I liberalism for having failed miserably in generating effective coordination by not recognizing that individuals are myopic and gullible, that competition in the marketplace is very imperfect, that public goods are never being produced in 'sufficient' quantity, that private enterprises are manipulative of the preferences of consumers and of the actions of elected and bureaucratic officials, and that the objectives of egalitarianism of outcome (regarded as the basic condition for the exercise of positive freedom) have not been fully realized.

Consequently, it was argued that the state had to take responsibility for the coordination work, for only this supra-individual entity could distill and come to embody the notion of public interest, and to ensure that the basic conditions for effective positive freedom (equality, rights, egalitarian distributive justice and the like) can be realized.

This was the *ad hoc* message of Keynes[6] in the face of the Great Depression, and the much more brutal message of

[5] *Stanford Encyclopedia of Philosophy, op.cit.*
[6] John Maynard Keynes. 1936. *The General Theory of Employment, Interest and Money.* New York, NY: Harcourt Brace.

Galbraith in denouncing the 'failures' of capitalist society in the post-World War II period.[7] This cosmology took hold in the 1930s as a countervailing state action to deal with the catastrophic Great Depression, but became a much more aggressive new gospel after the post World War II period, when significant intrusive state action became something that most citizens came to be persuaded that they were entitled to – in good as well as bad times – since the coordination problem was one that had to rest squarely on the shoulders of the state.

This drift from a state contribution to correcting abominable disruptions and unacceptable inequalities in periods of crisis, to the state being required by citizens, as a matter of perceived right, to provide insurance against all unpredictable duress, was consequential. This was the era when the array of claimed market failures (for which citizens felt entitled to compensation), and the claims for state support (supposedly required to ensure positive liberty), expanded exponentially. The welfare state led citizens to believe that their entitlement to be protected from any undesirable future was warranted and legitimate, and that the state was the only actor capable of ensuring that.

Type-II liberalism generated much criticism for its overambitious claim that the state would take responsibility for ensuring egalitarianism. This self-styled duty was shown to be a task often carried out in a wrong-headed way and, in any case, one that the state was most often not capable of carrying out.

Type-II liberalism showed very quickly that the promise of no-fault generalized insurance against all inconveniences was beyond its financial and operational capacities. In particular, a number of failures were revealed: the incapacity to deal with problems of evil (the vices of selfishness, greed, prejudice, laziness, etc.); the problem of eroding individual responsibility; the problem of distributive justice (rejecting 'deserving' as

---

[7] John Kenneth Galbraith. 1958. *The Affluent Society*. Boston, MA: Houghton-Mifflin; John Kenneth Galbraith. 1967. *The New Industrial State*. Boston, MA: Houghton-Mifflin.

a basis of justice); and the problem of pluralism (that type-II liberalism denies by insisting on a short list of basic shared values).[8] The immense amount of distortion introduced by massive and indiscriminate intrusive state intervention led to yet more coordination failures.

Type-II liberalism interpreted these additional coordination failures not as a consequence of heightened state intervention, but as a signal that immensely more State (now with a capital S) intervention was needed to correct these exponentially increasing state-generated coordination failures. This became the new gospel of the so-called welfare state, until the 1970s, when its gross flaws became glaringly apparent.

This was a period of stagflation, where the social rigidities generated by state interventions (and the formation of dense networks of collusive, cartelistic and lobbying organizations to influence state decisions) made it very difficult to revise downward the irresponsible social commitments that were translating into exponential cost increases at the time of a dramatic drop in productivity growth, because of a significant concomitant decline in personal responsibility.[9]

In the last few decades, a resurgence of type-I liberalism has ensued in Western democracies. But the countermove has been slow and painful for two reasons. First, the resilience of the *principe gouvernemental* (that leads uncommitted citizens to unload difficult problems onto the government, when that possibility exists, rather than dealing with them themselves); this significant flaw in our democratic political system had already been identified by Proudhon in the middle of the 19th century. And second, the noxious *pouvoir social*, denounced by Tocqueville, through which some of the intelligentsia and the media succeed in sacralizing (by systematic disinformation and ideological rants) the most ineffective social arrangements, and the most excessive entitlements,

---

[8] John Kekes. 1997. *Against Liberalism*. Ithaca, NY: Cornell University Press, chapter 10.

[9] Mancur Olson. 1982. *The Rise and Decline of Nations*. New Haven, CT: Yale University Press.

thereby making it difficult for those in authority to modify them.[10]

The reactions of the so-called 'progressives' to pressures to question social arrangements that are unduly generous and grossly inefficient have been strident. Any attempt to invoke with citizens the need for fiscal prudence, or more sense of responsibility, has been labeled 'neo-liberal' and retrograde, and tarred as challenging inviolable entitlements and *acquis*.

The mix of these three toxic ingredients (*le principe gouvernemental, un pouvoir social idéologiqué,* and the demagoguery of *l'évangile anti-néo-libéral* and the demonization of type-I liberalism) has made it very difficult to proceed in an orderly way with the normal continuous critical review of our current mode of governing.[11]

Limitations of these cosmologies in tackling the coordination problem

The citizenry in Western countries has grown somewhat uncomfortable with this Manichean world, in which one tribe argues vociferously for one panacea, and another equally vehemently for another. In fact, both sides represent crippling epistemologies rooted in unduly simplifying systems of belief that lead inquirers to posit certain assumptions as articles of faith and to choose tools or instruments of coordination (and to exclude others) on the basis of these assumptions. Since these assumptions are often questionable and empirically challengeable, dogmatic adherence to one approach or the other most often generates undesirable if not disastrous results, because the circumstances may demand hybrid arrangements to cope with baroque circumstances.

[10] François-Pierre Proudhon. 1851. *Confessions d'un révolutionnaire.* Paris, FR: Vrin; Daniel Innerarity. 2006. *La démocratie sans l'état.* Paris, FR: Climats; Raymond Boudon. 2005. *Tocqueville aujourd'hui.* Paris, FR: Odile Jacob.

[11] Gilles Paquet. 2011. *Tableau d'avancement II – Essais exploratoires sur la gouvernance d'un certain Canada français.* Ottawa, ON: Invenire, chapter 4.

The apostles of both cosmologies are, therefore, often prevented from taking advantage of the whole range of possible socio-economic arrangements by taboos and mental prisons – assumptions that, despite empirical evidence to the contrary, are regarded as canonical by one cosmology or the other.

The following table presents a sample of the idiosyncrasies of the two main cosmologies. This is not meant to be exhaustive, yet it captures the sharp differences in the *manières de voir* underpinning these two cosmologies, and reveals why they have become mental prisons, preventing the development of syntheses likely to provide better approaches to effective coordination.

Neither total reliance on the market and perfect competition, nor a total reliance on state planning and computation has emerged unscathed from the experiences of the late 20th century. When either approach began to dominate the scene, unintended consequences materialized that led to disappointments and to corrective action in the opposite direction. But the net effect of these movements back and forth did not have a neutral impact on the balance between these two cosmologies. The immense *pouvoir social* in support of the welfare state that has evolved over the last 60 years has tilted the equilibrium squarely in the direction of type-II liberalism, and has made statism the conventional wisdom.

TABLE 1

A Quick Sample of the Idiosyncrasies of the Two Ruling Cosmologies

	Type-I liberalism	Type-II liberalism
Individual	imperfectly informed	manipulated
Values	plural	shared
Priority	freedom	egalitarianism
Competition	rather perfect flexible prices	quite imperfect sticky prices
Interventionism	modest	robust
Time horizon	long term	short term
Trust	private > public	private < public
In charge	nobody	State
Information	scattered	in hand
G action	inquiring system	goals, control, marksmanship
Public service	interest group	new clergy

Despite the ruinous entitlements it has generated, and the personal irresponsibility it has engendered in the citizenry, type-II liberalism is the reference for most of the intelligentsia and the media in Canada, including Quebec, today. As a result of such disinformation and propaganda, a population that is not unaware that no wealth can be redistributed unless it has first been produced, and that increased productivity and innovation are rooted in personal initiative and imagination, has acquired a type-II entitlement mentality, and has suppressed any *malaise* about the philosophy of always demanding more, while being willing to contribute less.

The population's state of mind is somewhat schizophrenic. There is a vague general awareness of the need to produce wealth in order to gain access to the high standard of living to which the citizens aspire (based on type-I liberalism), but this awareness is completely overshadowed and obliterated by a sense of entitlement that is overpowering and appears falsely legitimate because it is couched in the language of rights (type-II liberalism).

The way to maintain sanity in the face of such schizophrenic views is not to reflect on one's own irresponsibility or lack of productivity (which would produce much anxiety and some behavioural adjustment), but to ascribe the failures of the socio-economic system to the abuses and excesses of certain producers of wealth, to cling staunchly to the belief that each citizen has a fundamental right to share the wealth, whoever produces it, and to claim that enforcing this entitlement transcends all other duties of the state.

This static view of wealth sharing (occluding any concern about the impact of indiscriminate wealth redistribution on wealth production) of type-II liberalism is in stark contradiction with the dynamic view of wealth production that underpins type-I liberalism, but this static view is the one in good currency.

In the past, only major disasters (wars, revolutions, etc.) forcing a shakedown of the vested interests (and a questioning of their dogmas) have been able to rekindle the dynamics of productivity and innovation in modern advanced economies.[12] In a world mired in entitlement mentality, cognitive dissonance generates blindness and blocks out any capacity for critical thinking about dysfunctional arrangements until crisis time, as the recent European experience suggests.

The rise and evolution of the notion of governance

Over the past 30 years, there has been much dissatisfaction with the two ruling cosmologies having trapped the debates in the doldrums of hierarchy + state *versus* markets + networks. In the case of public administration, it was traditional public administration *versus* new public management. Consequently, debates stumbled from Charybdis to Scylla, or the other way around. This could hardly be expected to carry the discussion forward.

---

[12] Charles P. Kindleberger. 1978. *The Aging Economy*. Kiel, Germany: Institut für Weltwirtschaft.

What was not acknowledged is what can be regarded as the contextual changes that have been responsible for making both these cosmologies appear quite defective:

1. power, resources and information have become more and more widely dispersed into a variety of hands;
2. the environments have become more turbulent and the practices more varied, the texture of our societies more complex and plural, and the processes and interactions have come to mobilize a greater variety of stakeholders, holding very different views and generating, therefore, more and more dilemmas; and
3. there has been much greater relevant uncertainty and greater difficulty in generating the requisite knowledge to navigate effectively in these stormy seas; this baroque and turbulent context does not seem tractable with the simple mechanisms proposed by either of the two traditional cosmologies.

What is required are hybrid arrangements combining all sorts of mechanisms that might have proved useful in different sectors at different times – new practices and organizational designs (multi-jurisdictional, hybrid, plural), operating as inquiring systems, and generating the equivalent of automatic pilots (to borrow a metaphor) to probe this ever changing environment and to ensure the requisite stewardship.[13]

This can only mean exorcizing the mythical 'invisible hand' of market and perfect competition, and unpacking the equally opaque notion of 'state' and perfect computation, and squarely facing the challenge of institutional and organizational design. I cannot hope to undertake such a Herculean task in this short book, but I intend at least to underline three trends that have been widely acknowledged over the last few decades, but that have not been sufficiently heralded in our northern kingdom.

---

[13] Gilles Paquet. 2009. *Scheming virtuously – The road to collaborative governance*. Ottawa, ON: Invenire; Mark Bevir (ed.). 2011. *The Sage Handbook of Governance*. Los Angeles, CA: Sage.

From Big 'G' to small 'g', reluctantly

As early as the 1990s,[14] the drift from Big 'G' government (hierarchical, centralizing, homogenizing) toward small 'g' governance (open, non-centralizing, pluralistic, distributed) had been observed in the private, public and social sectors, and had led to a shift away from oversight-heavy forms of governing to a more decentred, collaborative and partnership-based governing in Canada and elsewhere.

This drift had been triggered by a two-step crisis:

- *a crisis in the economic realm*, revealed from the 1970s by more and more important coordination failures in advanced market economies (stagflation, etc.); and
- *a crisis of the state*, which was failing to mobilize the requisite commitment of citizens to do the jobs required, and to obtain a blank cheque from the citizenry to do whatever was necessary. Most citizens, even though their expectations in terms of entitlements from the state had grown exponentially over the last few decades, had become strangely unwilling to provide the commitment of emotional, intellectual and financial resources to ensure the continuous refurbishment of the public infrastructure. This could only lead to demand overload. The frustration generated by the policy failures of the 1970s set the stage for suggestions that the best way to strengthen both democracy and the economy was to weaken the state.[15]

The state, in the past, had played housekeeping roles and offsetting functions, so these functions required minimal input from the citizenry. But the state in modern, complex, advanced economies has played new central roles that have gone much beyond these mechanical interventions, and had to become involved as a broker and as a partner in participatory planning, if the requisite organizational learning was to

[14] Gilles Paquet. 1999. "Innovations in Governance in Canada," *www. optimumonline.ca*, 29(2/3): 71-81.

[15] Gilles Paquet. 1999. *Governance Through Social Learning*. Ottawa, ON: The University of Ottawa Press, chapter 11.

materialize. This led to the need for new design principles for the governing apparatus.

The citizen has become reluctantly and very slowly more and more forced to realize that he could not remain a passive beneficiary, but would have to become a co-producer of governance. This triggered a very slow move away from a culture of entitlements and *egalitarianism stricto sensu* (the general top-down thrust that underpinned the welfare state) toward a philosophy of *subsidiarity* (according to which power should be devolved to the lowest, most local level at which decisions can reasonably be made). Indeed, the six questions on which the Program Review process within the federal government of the mid-1990s in Canada was based were all about subsidiarity although the word was never used.[16]

This new philosophy has provided a rationale for the construction of a new institutional order, where governance would be based on needs rather than rights, and bottom-up rather than top-down. It would also be more distributed and more decentralized than the old governance system. This drift from Big 'G' to small 'g' has translated, in the case of Canada, into a variety of initiatives like airport administration being devolved to the local level, for instance.[17] But there has been an immense amount of inertia in Canadian society, and this drift toward small 'g' governance has proceeded at a snail's pace as a result of what some would call malignant narcissim.[18]

The three waves

Obviously, the general drift from Big 'G' to small 'g' has proceeded at an uneven pace, depending on the context. But in general, it has unfolded in three waves, identified by Bevir and

[16] Gilles Paquet. 2005. *Gouvernance: une invitation à la subversion*. Montreal, QC: Liber, chapter XV.

[17] Gilles Paquet. 1999. "Innovations in Governance ..." *op.cit.*, 76ff.

[18] There is no doubt that Canada is failing to respond effectively and creatively to a number of basic challenges created by the old welfare state and its philosophy of entitlements. This dynamic conservatism has slowed down considerably the evolution toward active subsidiarity and small 'g' governance. Robin Higham and Gilles Paquet. 2013. "Reflections on the Canadian Malaise," *www.optimumonline.ca*, 43(2): 1-12.

Rhodes as the emergence of *network governance, metagovernance* and *decentred governance.*[19]

According to Bevir and Rhodes, the first wave came in response to the challenges of failure-prone, top-down hierarchical bureaucratic governing, as governance became associated with a greater use of markets, quasi-markets, networks and alternative program deliveries in the 1980s. This led to a certain erosion of the citadel of the state and to an awareness that things could be done differently. But in countries like Canada, the state bureaucracy was able to mount a robust resistance movement, to demonize and slow this search for alternative mechanisms. Ambitious plans were deliberately stunted.[20] As a result, the state maintained its *dominium* in Canada more than in many other countries. This propaganda was accompanied by dire warnings about the hollowing out of the state: the citizen was warned that fragmentation would prevail, networks would become the dominant coordinating mechanisms, and there would inexorably be a weakened and softer central state control, if any.[21]

The second wave saw a slowing down of the resistance movement (at least on the surface), and what appeared to be an acceptance of the drift away from bureaucracy toward markets and networks, and an acceptance of the fact that the spectre of the hollowing out of the state had been overplayed. Metagovernance became the rallying call, and the label by which to refer to the new form of indirect steering of more relatively autonomous stakeholders. The state apparatus realized that it had not lost its power, but that it would have to exercise it in a more subtle and oblique way: securing coordination by negotiation, diplomacy and the like. Thereby,

[19] Mark Bevir and R.A.W. Rhodes. 2010. *The State as Cultural Practice.* Oxford, UK: Oxford University Press, chapter 5.

[20] Gilles Paquet. 1997. "Alternative Program Delivery: Transforming the Practices of Governance", in Robin Ford and David Zussman (eds.). *Alternative Service Delivery: Sharing Governance in Canada.* Toronto, ON: IPAC/ KPMG, p. 31-58.

[21] R.A.W. Rhodes. 1997. *Understanding Governance.* Buckingham, UK: Open University Press.

it would still remain in a position to quarterback the system by designing a combination of hierarchical, market and network governance.[22] In its more devious incarnation, this wave would welcome diverse forms of 'governmentality' *à la* Foucault, i.e., working at persuading the citizen to welcome his own voluntary submission to the will of the state.[23]

The third wave has challenged the idea that there is anything inexorable about either some hollowing out of the state or some emergence of a new form of indirect steering by the state – with no social logic determining one outcome or the other.

What is becoming evident is *de facto* a collaborative 'decentred metagovernance' that recognizes that the outcome in our chaotic world is that multiple stakeholders will create a contingent pattern of rules through their diverse understandings and conflicting actions.[24] Bevir and Rhodes announced the arrival of the stateless state as the contingent product of the diverse actions, practices and struggles informed by the beliefs of the stakeholders. They also suggest a focus on the stories and narratives of the different stakeholders as a way to unpack that notion of stateless state.

It is possible to agree wholeheartedly with Bevir and Rhodes about the non-inexorability of the outcomes propounded by the first and second wave, without being swayed by their conclusion that the total contingency of the outcome of the drift from Big 'G' to small 'g' amounts to pure randomness. Nor is the hermeneutic solution out of the conundrum, *à la* Bevir-Rhodes, the only way.

There may be a third way between positivism and hermeneutics.

---

[22] Bob Jessop. 2007. *State Power.* Cambridge, UK: Polity; Louis Meuleman. 2008. *Public Management and the Metagovernance of Hierarchies, Networks and Markets.* Heidelberg, Germany: Physica-Verlag.

[23] Gilles Paquet. 2008. *Gouvernance: mode d'emploi.* Montreal, QC: Liber, chapter 2.

[24] Mark Bevir and R.A.W. Rhodes. 2010. *op.cit.,* 90ff.

The Quantum notion of governance

What has been challenged by the third wave is not the existence of order, but the existence of a mechanistic Newtonian order, as ordained in the traditional analyses. What has been experienced over the last while is the emergence of something akin to a Quantum order – arrangements that would not appear to be following simple causal and easily predictable paths, but arrangements about which one can only make statistical assertions and invoke probability clouds. There may be a certain degree of indeterminacy, but there is an underpinning order that does *not* depend on someone being totally in charge.

The traditional cosmologies in good currency in the social sciences have a Newtonian flavour. The world is presented as a set of mechanical and predictable objects, as a whole that is no more than the sum of its parts, capable of being broken down into component parts that can be studied piecemeal, and can be "understood through rational inquiry based on objectivity, certainty and chain reasoning ... It is based on certainty, order, structure, status and determinism."[25] This is the vision of the world that underpins the 'goals-and-control' view of public policy and the ideology of type-II liberalism.

It is, therefore, quite natural for approaches based on such Newtonian thinking to embrace the idea of metagovernance (the state hijacking control through indirect means). But some recent work has shown that this is too simplistic. Inquiring systems and social learning by various different stakeholders in robust interaction question the fable of the state being the only actor capable of metagoverning action. Any stakeholder with a portion of the resources, power and information may be able to nudge the organization or the social system by indulging in some metagovernance, i.e., some redesign of arrangements of diverse sorts. Indeed, collaborative decentred metagovernance (opening metagoverning action to all stakeholders and to

[25] Christa Daryl Slaton. 1991. "Quantum Theory and Political Theory" in Theodore L. Becker (ed.). *Quantum Politics – Applying Quantum Theory to Political Phenomena*. New York, NY: Praeger, p. 42-43.

collaborative efforts) would appear to be much more likely to
elicit a sort of guidance – or automatic pilot – capable of ensuring
continuous learning and an evolving stewardship apparatus.[26]

But the way in which this type of coordination materializes,
under a collaborative decentred governance regime, cannot be
expressed meaningfully in Newtonian terms because certainty
and determinism are no longer the order of the day.

The corollaries of the Newtonian assumptions are well-
known and widely accepted by conventional social scientists:
individualism (humans as separate and self-contained);
hedonistic psychology (motivations are precise, rational and
predictable); equality (each human being is commensurable
and interchangeable); mutual exclusivity (humans cannot
occupy the same place at the same time without conflict and
power relations ensuing), and each human pursuing his
own self-interest in this individualistic dog-eat-dog world.[27]
Moreover, it is presumed that, through some not-always-
well-understood processes, leaders can distil the 'aggregate
preferences' of their deferent or fearful followers and rationally
guide the organization or the social system in keeping with
these guideposts.

These assumptions are highly contestable. Humans are
most often best defined by their environment and relationships,
rather than by their innate preferences; their desires, intentions,
and talents are unequal; they share space and collaborate;
their behaviour is not determined only by external stimuli,
but also by discourse, deliberation and herd movements; and
the individual-ranked preferences cannot be aggregated into a
consistent community-wide ranking.[28]

The Newtonian world is too simplistic, too absolute and
too limited to be able to provide a useful representation of our
complex and turbulent world. The pretence, for instance, that

[26] Ruth Hubbard, Gilles Paquet and Christopher Wilson. 2012. *Stewardship: Collaborative Decentred Metagovernance and Inquiring Systems*. Ottawa, ON: Invenire, chapter 1.
[27] Christa Daryl Slaton, *op.cit.*, p. 45-47; Benjamin Barber. 1984. *Strong Democracy*. Berkeley, CA: The University of California Press.
[28] Christa Daryl Slaton, *op.cit.*, p. 48; Benjamin Barber, *op.cit.*, p. 42.

the state can elicit transcendent commonly-agreed-upon values that would serve as guideposts, is pure fantasy. This has greatly crippled the traditional approaches to governing organizations and social systems, to the point where some have referred to traditional political science as an "antiquarian discipline"[29] and indicted the social sciences as seemingly trapped in a stage of development that is not unlike the state of biology when it classified animals according to the number of legs.

The idea that anyone can know reality in all its details is fiction. Traditional and mechanical notions of rationality and cause-effect determinism are also unduly simplistic. So the chasms between such simplified representations and the full richness of experience is increasingly bound to force the social sciences (and political science, in particular) to abandon their cartoonesque representations and adopt a more sensible set of representations, based on a sort of Quantum perspective.

In the Quantum world, the major principles are quite different:

- objects are defined by their environments and their relationships with others;
- cause-effect determinism and rational decision making are not at the root of all human interactions;
- human systems are dynamic, moving processes that most often cannot be divided into discrete units for analysis; and
- there is no objective real world apart from one's consciousness.

The Quantum perspective recognizes that human beings are unpredictable and contradictory in nature, that it is often impossible to determine cause and effect except in probabilistic terms, that in the process of social learning and collaboration that underpin human activities much is to be ascribed to beliefs and emotions.

This entails a redefinition of rationality as ecological fit, and of the policy process as inquiring and wayfinding systems –

[29] Glendon A. Schubert. 1983. "The Evolution of Political Science: Paradigms of Physics, Biology and Politics," *Politics and The Life Sciences*, (1): 98.

freed from the naïveties of assuming that rationality is simple internal coherence, and of the caricatures of the policy/strategy process as goal-control and bow-arrow-target contraptions, as suggested by the traditional paradigm.

Obviously, this calls for revisiting many assumptions in good currency, for modifying the vocabulary used to define the problems, for adding key concepts to the intellectual tool box, and for reconceiving the whole dynamics of stewardship of human systems on the basis of fundamental uncertainty, limited information, experimentation, social learning and continuous interactions that modify the very settings of the game. Moreover, the broader megacommunity, the powerful impact of the environment, and the forces of self-organization must be seriously taken into account as forces of co-governance.

John G. Heilman has provided a most interesting survey of past and living social scientists who were quite conscious of those challenges, and has shown (as illustration) how the institutional analysis of Elinor Ostrom (a recent Nobel prize winner in economics) is based on a conceptual framework that has factored in comprehensiveness, recursiveness and creativity by adopting a Quantum perspective in her research.[30] One might say the same thing about the work of Charles Sabel.[31]

Not all participants in the conversations about stewardship, collaborative decentred metagovernance and inquiring systems agree on all aspects of this dramatic paradigm shift, on the central importance of the same particular assumptions or of the same key concepts as mental tools, nor hold the same view about the nexus of forces shaping the stewardship of organizations and social systems, and thus about the most effective ways to nudge organizations and social systems in desirable directions. But they all agree

---

[30] John G. Heilman. 1991. "Present at the Creation: A Quantum Perspective on the Methodology of Political Research" in Theodore L. Becker, *op.cit*. p. 201-219; Elinor Ostrom. 2005. *Understanding Institutional Diversity*. Princeton, NJ: Princeton University Press.

[31] Charles F. Sabel. 2001. "A Quiet Revolution of Democratic Governance: Towards Democratic Experimentalism" in Wolfgang Michalski et al. *Governance in the 21st Century*. Paris, FR: OECD.

that changes in the mindset and in the *outillage mental* will have to accompany the shift from views associated with the traditional Newtonian cosmology to the Quantum views aligned with collaborative decentred metagovernance.

Experiments at the Centre on Governance

The Bevir and Rhodes approach questions the very essence, structural quality and power of the state. This is their notion of stateless state – "a state that consists solely of contingent practices." This sort of approach is likely to be regarded as intrinsically heretical by most traditional political scientists and public administration professors and practitioners – for whom the state is "an almost monolithic entity able to act by making policy or undertaking metagovernance." For Bevir and Rhodes, the state is "merely an aggregate descriptive term for a vast array of meaningful actions that coalesce into contingent, shifting, and contested practices."[32]

Organization theorists have seized the challenges defined by collaborative decentred metagovernance. This has led to the production of a number of genuine alternatives to the stale and ineffective traditional public administration model, and not only to a simple application of the approach suggested by Bevir and Rhodes.

One such alternative, developed at the Centre on Governance of the University of Ottawa,[33] has been built on the fact that power, resources, knowledge and information are widely dispersed among many stakeholders. Consequently, the very notion of leadership or anyone in charge has been challenged, and the notions of policy and strategy have been replaced by the notion of an inquiring system at the core of collaborative decentred metagovernance.

This puts organizational design at centre stage: the design of mechanisms to mop up all the relevant information and

---

[32] Bevir and Rhodes, 2010, *op.cit.*, p. 198.
[33] For an overview of the work that led to this approach, see Gilles Paquet. 2009. *Scheming virtuously, op.cit*; for an outline of the ways in which the collaborative decentred metagovernance can be used, see Ruth Hubbard, Gilles Paquet and Christopher Wilson, 2012, *Stewardship, op.cit.*

knowledge, to generate the sort of wayfinding process ensuring resilience and innovation through the highest and best use of all sorts of heuristics and affordances to improve coordination and to ensure, thereby, the requisite collaboration for effective stewardship.

The key feature of this process is that it is no longer the monopoly of the state nor of the 'Great Leader' to metagovern. It is anchored in the variety of initiatives that stakeholders and partners can instantiate to nudge the organization in desirable ways. What emerges is, of necessity, contingent on the pattern of these initiatives, and on the ways in which they interact with one another, with the complex and turbulent environment, and with the forces of self-organization.

Collaborative decentred metagovernance is obviously not deterministic, but it is not pure white noise either. There are patterns that can be detected as more promising than others, and ways in which they can be made more probable.

In the study of certain issue domains, it has been shown that effective inquiring systems have been nudged into place by collaboration that often started with simple information sharing,[34] and evolved into an *avventura comune* based on nothing more than "concord" (homonoia – "a relationship between people who are not strangers, between whom goodwill is possible, but not friendship, ... a relationship based on respect ... for differences").[35]

Such patterns of collaboration may fail, so there is a need for fail-safe mechanisms. But they may also develop much beyond the stage of concord into genuine *affectio societatis* – a trust and commitment that allows collaboration to proceed much further.[36] It most often crystallizes *par morceaux*, but may also develop in a virus-like manner so as to encompass broad organizational segments of society.

---

[34] This has been the case in ocean governance, see Gilles Paquet. 2005. *The New Geo-Governance: A Baroque Approach*. Ottawa, ON: The University of Ottawa Press, part III.

[35] Gilles Paquet. 1999. *Governance Through Social Learning, op.cit., p.* 203; Adrian Oldfield. 1990. *Citizenship and Community*. London, UK: Routledge.

[36] Vincent Cuisinier. 2008. *L'affectio societatis*. Montpellier, FR: Litec.

This approach has been applied to a variety of cases with considerable success (medical journals, city-regions, the RCMP, multicultural accommodation, etc.).[37] Yet these successes in demonstrating the feasibility and effectiveness of alternative forms of such collaborative decentred metagovernance have not shaken the indefectible faith of the guardians of the old-style public administration in the State, and their indomitable support for type-II liberalism in Canada.

This cultural lag of Canadian public administration has been nurtured to a very great extent by its immensely conservative DNA – a fabric that has kept alive the myths of the transcendental nature of the State, of its capacity to immunize against all undesirable outcomes, and of state bureaucrats as a new clergy whose work must not, under any consideration, be devolved to lay personnel.[38]

Conclusion

The struggle between type-I and type-II liberalism (market *versus* state) continues unabated, and the bias in favour of statism remains strong both among most of the intelligentsia and the public service in Canada.

The statist position is so deeply ingrained that the intelligentsias do not even explore the third way opened by the world of governance. Governance is not taught in most schools of public administration. One should therefore not expect that the academic branch of Canadian public administration will be the source of any conceptual refurbishment.

As for the practitioners of public administration, governance is regarded as a case of *lèse-majesté* in government circles. Even evidence of gross inefficiency (for instance, that the pay system of the federal public service in Canada costs 15 times more per employee to operate than the industry standard[39] leaves them unperturbed. Indeed, an extensive

[37] Gilles Paquet. 2008. *Gouvernance: mode d'emploi*. Montreal, QC: Liber, part III.
[38] Gilles Paquet. 2012. "Slouching toward a relatively stateless state," *www. optimumonline.ca*, 42(2): 99-121.
[39] Don Mazankowski and Paul Tellier et al. 2009. *Third Report of the Prime Minister's Advisory Committee on the Public Service*. Ottawa, ON: Privy Council Office.

series of seminars with senior public servants in Ottawa has revealed that over recent years a grievous lack of critical thinking has developed in the public service.[40] It would appear that only once senior executives have retired or left the public service do they occasionally restore active use of their critical senses and denounce the immensely flawed governing practices they have observed while on guard for us.[41]

[40] Ruth Hubbard and Gilles Paquet. 2010. *The Black Hole of Public Administration*. Ottawa, ON: The University of Ottawa Press, chapter 3.
[41] Ian Clark and Harry Swain. 2005. "Distinguishing the Real and the Surreal in Management Reform: Suggestions from Beleaguered Administrators in the Government of Canada," *Canadian Public Administration*, 48(4): 453-476.

CHAPTER 2

| Governance as Mythbuster

"Most organizations would rather risk obsolescence
than make room for the non-conformists in their midst."

Warren Bennis

Introduction

The notion of governance has been in use since the 13th century, but it has had a dramatic resurgence in public usage over the last few decades. This is ascribable to a new configuration of circumstances that has called for a new word to capture an emerging reality.

These new circumstances (generated by globalization, accelerated technical change, more extensive intercontinental demographic shuffles and greater cultural diversity in particular sites, etc.) have resulted in a much richer and more complex socio-political texture in our socio-economies. This has generated more and more *wicked* problems – i.e., problems where the goals are either not known or are very ambiguous, and the means-ends relationships are highly uncertain and poorly understood. Consequently, these wicked problems call for the design of a variety of new and ever more sophisticated governing arrangements to cope with them.[1]

---

[1] Gilles Paquet. 1999. "Tackling Wicked Problems" in G. Paquet, *Governance Through Social Learning*. Ottawa, ON: The University of Ottawa Press, p. 41-52.

To deal with such complex issues and ill-structured problems, the conventional approach to strategy and policy has proven quite inadequate. These issues do not lend themselves *ab ovo* to a precise problem definition; the resources, power and information necessary to define the problems, and to design suitable responses are not in the hands, head and soul of a single authority; and any effective response to such problems is dependent on collaboration from many individuals and groups in the *megacommunity*.[2]

Such a setting does not lend itself to the conventional management science approach in private, public or social organizations – an approach which presumes that organizations are *governed* by a leader who has a good understanding of the environment, of its future trends if nothing is done to modify it, of the inexorable rules of the game one has to put up with, and of the goals pursued by the organization. Such a Newtonian approach assumes a world of deterministic, well-behaved processes where causality is mechanically simple. Coordination is consequently trivialized: building on the supposedly well-defined goals of the organization and mechanical causality, the leader chooses supposedly apt control mechanisms likely to get the organization where its leader wants it to be, and programmed followers follow.

There are, no doubt, many issues that are still amenable to this simplistic approach. But as the pace of change accelerates, and as the issues grow more complex, private, public and social organizations are confronted with more and more wicked problems that require elucidation through exploratory inquiry. A meaningful *inquiry* (in the Deweyan sense) can only mean "thinking and acting that originates in and aims at resolving a situation of uncertainty, doubt and

[2] A megacommunity is defined as a collaborative socio-economic environment in which business, government and civil society interact according to their own common interests while maintaining their unique priorities (Mark Gerencser et al. 2008. *Megacommunities*. New York, NY: Palgrave Macmillan, p. 232).

puzzlement."[3] This calls for a new way of thinking about governing. At best, organizations can only govern themselves by becoming capable of learning both what their goals are, and the means to reach them, *as they proceed*. This is done by tapping into the widely distributed knowledge and information in possession of the many, mobilizing the power and resources that potential members and partners have, and getting them to collectively invent ways to collaboratively work themselves out of the predicaments in which they are, collectively.

The notion of *governance* – as effective coordination when power, resources and information are widely distributed into many hands, heads and souls – acquires then a different and much broader connotation than the notion of *government* that has become roughly associated only with the conventional top-down approach to governing.

Such a notion of governance has acquired a *subversive reputation*, has challenged perspectives in good currency, and has generated much hostility on both the left and the right of the ideological spectrum. For instance, in the public sector, the ideologues on the left (*the progressive*) have perceived governance as challenging the state-centric view of the world they hold dear, while the ideologues on the right (*the conservative*) have interpreted it as a potential subterfuge to furtively introduce a form of *coercion lite* that they are most uncomfortable with. In the private and social sectors, governance – bringing the meaningful stakeholders centre stage – has also generated the same sort of mixed feelings from the hypercentralizers and the hyperdecentralizers.

Additional hostility was generated when it was fully realized that the governance-approach's challenge of the ruling ideologies calls for revisiting many notions to which the public had become accustomed (leadership, strategy/policy, accountability, etc.). As a result, governance has been shunned

[3] Donald A. Schön. 1995. "Causality and Causal Inference in the Study of Organizations" in R.F. Goodman and W.R. Fisher (eds.). *Rethinking Knowledge*. Albany, NY: State University of New York, p. 69-101 (citation on p. 82).

and denounced as useless, ideological and toxic.[4] And even when the governance approach has had, most reluctantly, to be ever so slightly accommodated because of the accumulation of evidence that mauled the traditional perspectives, it has been dramatically emasculated and transmogrified to fit well within the set of presumptions in good currency.[5]

This chapter proceeds in four stages. First, it presents a stylized version of the governance approach. Second, it shows how this approach transforms key concepts in use. Third, it questions the persiflage about the governance approach by various groups most reluctant to reframe their view of the world. Fourth, it puts forward conjectures about the evolution of governance studies.

The governance approach

The governance approach is built on the discomfort generated by two foundational myths on which the conventional *Big 'G' (government) approach* is built:

- *Myth #1* – that, in public, private and social organizations, someone has all the power, resources and information to take full charge; and
- *Myth #2* – that such 'higher authority' takes action in policy and strategy on the basis of common or shared values.

---

[4] Gilles Paquet. 2011. *Gouvernance: un antimanuel.* Montreal, QC: Liber, chapter 1.

[5] Having to modify one's frame of reference is never easy. This is all the more difficult when one is pressed to abandon highly stylized canonical views that have been in good currency for decades, to embrace a *problematique* which is still in the making, in the process of being developed. This is a phenomenon that has been observed every time an old established paradigm has been challenged by a new and emerging one. This explains why the notion of governance was sanitized by the World Bank when the issue first percolated. Good governance was ordained to mean nothing more than eliminating corruption. The problem was also cannibalized by accountants, financiers and lawyers – for whom it has been reduced to the principal-agent problem, and to the machinations of boardrooms, or the fancifulness of transparency and *ex post* accountability. These reductive reactions are understandable, but that does not make them less disastrous.

As suggested above, in our complex socio-economic world, private, public and social organizations most often cannot be presumed to be operating under the authority of a single omniscient and omnipotent 'leader', governing in the name of common or shared values. An alternative and more satisfactory paradigm – the *small 'g' (governance) approach* – would suggest that organizations operate under the guidance of an assemblage of partners, equipped with quite different values and purposes, who each have a portion of the power, the resources and information, and who hopefully may find ways to agree on certain principles and norms for conducting their business in a manner that is in keeping with their respective, yet different, appreciative systems, allowing for ways of *vivre-ensemble* that promise to generate effectiveness, resilience and innovation.

The small 'g' governance approach raises some fundamental questions that are never confronted head-on by the Big 'G' government approach because they are wrongly presumed to be already resolved. There is a need to find ways:

(A) to ensure effective coordination among the quite different parties who have a significant portion of the power, resources and information required to steer the organization; and

(B) to arrive at agreed upon principles and norms of *vivre-ensemble* (regimes of engagement) as a *modus operandi* to ensure effective stewardship of the organization.

These two tasks are daunting, and they depend on the development of a *coordination science* that has not, up to now, received anything like the attention it requires.

The conventional wisdom (presuming that someone is in charge, and that shared values ensure the requisite guideposts) has failed and, as a result, governing has faltered in all sectors, as revealed by a variety of indicators of productivity and innovation. Small 'g' (governance) has not, however, magically ensured that effective coordinating arrangements among the stakeholders and principles of *vivre-ensemble* have always materialized in perfect form. In the recent past, governance studies have only sharpened and clarified what we know about the process of governing in the real world,[6] and have proposed ways to tackle tasks A and B referred to above.

Stewardship and the Detox Prism

A sample of this work might be two recent books published under the auspices of the Centre on Governance.[7]

The first one examined how the process of stewardship in private, public and social organizations escapes from the traditional bow-arrow-target marksmanship framework of the traditional Big 'G' *problematique*, through redefining policy and strategy as *inquiring systems*. It defines the way in which the inquiring system crystallizes through experimentation with prototypes. An inquiring system elicits the way in which organizations redefine, as they learn, both the hard (architecture and routines) and soft (culture, behaviour, principles, etc.) dimensions of the *automatic pilot* (if I may be allowed this metaphor). And so they steer and nudge the organization along, in the face of a surprise-generating environment and evolving interactions.

Explored in the book (both conceptually and through cases) is a sample of mechanisms that have proven extremely useful in stewarding organizations in the private, public and social sectors, and which are at the core of governance repairs. For instance,

- the setting up of ever more inclusive forums for effective multilogue;
- the negotiation of moral contracts defining well, yet informally, the mutual expectations of the different partners;

[6] Much work has been done over the last 15 years in many laboratories – of which the Centre on Governance (co-sponsored by the Telfer School of Management and the Faculty of Social Sciences at the University of Ottawa) is one. Over 50 books have been produced under the auspices of the Centre since the late 1990s.

[7] Ruth Hubbard, Gilles Paquet and Christopher Wilson. 2012. *Stewardship: Collaborative Decentred Metagovernance and Inquiring Systems*. Ottawa, ON: Invenire; Gilles Paquet and Tim Ragan. 2012. *Through the Detox Prism: Exploring Organizational Failures and Design Responses*. Ottawa, ON: Invenire.

- the design of learning loops, enabling the partners to revise their choices of means as the experience unfolds, but also enabling them to revise the very objectives pursued through reframing the organization and its very mission when that proves necessary; and
- the invention of fail-safe mechanisms to ensure that the multilogue does not degenerate into meaningless consensuses or stalemates, and to prevent *saboteurs* from derailing the collective effort.

The second book identifies five important interfaces (within organizations, and between organizations and their contexts) where most of the coordination failures materialize, probing the proximate sources of dysfunction at these five interfaces. Between the organization and:

- its employees (x-inefficiency);
- its value chain upstream (the opacity of the value chain allowing the escape from fault);
- its socio-physical environment (externalities);
- its governance regime (allowing hijacking by certain groups);
- its ethical context (moral vacancy).

Toxicities at these five interfaces are interrelated, and are at the source of something like two-thirds to three-quarters of the observed social waste. The inquiry, built around the detox prism, gauges the toxicity at these five interfaces, probes their sources, and suggests families of design repairs based on a mix of mechanisms of practical use in the different sectors.

This detox perspective is based on a systematic effort to lift both analysts and practitioners to a higher perspective point in order to broaden their outlook, to lengthen their time horizons, to help them escape from the conventional mental prisons, and to inspire effective and practical design thinking.

The various chapters illustrate how good design thinking can help to repair these coordination failures through the right mix of *incentive reward systems* and *moral contracts and conventions* – that can shape the stewardship (or the nexus of mechanisms making up the guiding system) in such a way as to promote effective coordination and collaboration, as well as the resilience of the organization, social learning, innovation, and progress.

Four key notions transformed in the small 'g' world

In the sort of Quantum world of small 'g' (governance), the ground is in motion, nothing is deterministic, and objects are defined by their environments. In this world, no single force fully dominates the governance regime. Depending on the moment or the site, the governance regime will succeed to a greater or lesser degree in generating stewardship that ensures resilience and innovation for the organization. This new perspective challenges some very basic concepts on which the Big 'G' (government) world is based. This is not the place to review the whole panoply of concepts made obsolete (or somewhat modified) as a result of this tectonic shift, but we can at least illustrate how four central notions have thereby been transformed – strategy/policy, leadership, accountability and evaluation.

Strategy/policy and leadership

In the traditional Big 'G' cosmology, it is presumed that someone is in possession of all the information, power and resources to guide the organization or the social system in choosing directions defined by shared values. In this assumed Newtonian world, strategy and policy entail nothing more than the design of a control system that will ensure the realization of the agreed upon objectives, in the manner stylized by management science after World War II.

The small 'g' perspective is anchored in a more realistic appreciation of the real-world situation, in all its imprecision and complexity: ill-structured problems, power, resources and information widely distributed among many hands and heads, no agreement on shared values in a plural and pluralist society, and a turbulent and surprise-generating environment that is continually changing.

In such circumstances, there is no way of meaningfully imposing *ab ovo* a problem definition and precise targets, and an algorithm to reach those precise targets. The only way to tackle the issue is to design an *exploratory inquiring system* that can distill its goals and means by trial and error as learning proceeds. What is required to do this is an exploration engine capable of eliciting *effective wayfinding* through constant reconfiguration of the perspective, as the environment evolves, and experience accumulates. The inquiring system is not only searching for the *most promising path* to the evolving objectives, but also (and concomitantly) the *most promising alliances* of relevant and useful partners, and the *most promising ways to motivate them* to coordinate their actions and to contribute to this collective task. It is from this sort of inquiry that a constant redefinition of the problem can be expected and the sort of social learning likely to generate resilience and innovation.

In this small 'g' world, the notions of strategy and policy are in the nature of dynamic searches for elusive and changing missions, and have become much fuzzier and more imprecise than in the world of Big 'G'.[8]

The first victim of this transformation of the notions of strategy and policy is the notion of leadership. If no one is in charge (contrary to what is presumed in the Big 'G' world), the notion of personalized leadership becomes much less meaningful. It has to be replaced by a much different notion of *stewardship* – a continually evolving assemblage of mechanisms making up the sort of automatic pilot that steers the organization, more or less collegially, in ways likely to generate effective wayfinding through effective self-refurbishment.

This is why governance is so subversive, and generates such strong reactions from all those who claim to be in charge: for them, it is imperative to defend and legitimize 'leadership' as a matter of their own survival. Consequently, an enormous

---

[8] Gilles Paquet and Christopher Wilson. 2011. "Collaborative Co-governance as Inquiring Systems," *www.optimumonline.ca*, 41(2): 1-12.

literature has arisen in the last decades to attempt to rescue the notion of leadership from its *deliquescence*.[9]

Accountability and evaluation

Ex post hard punitive accountability, almost exclusively based on quantitative financial metrics, was celebrated in earlier times as a way to ensure discipline and control, but this has become less and less highly regarded in the new turbulent and complex world in which we live. It is too reductive and myopic, and too likely to elicit both scapegoats (in circumstances where blame cannot and should not be easily attributed) and some deterrence of experimentation.

Transparency, quantophrenia and punishment are not panaceas, and in any case they cannot suffice. What is called for is a reframing of the notion of accountability in a manner that ensures that:

- all the relevant stakeholders are fully engaged and held responsible, and
- all the important standards (or *grandeurs*, or dimensions of interest) they live by are evoked in the creative dialogue and the creative practice from which the viable compromises emerge.

This means a 360-degree accountability among partners: accountability that takes into account various gauges of performance, is *forward-looking, exploratory and experimentalist in focus*, and feeds effective and creative social learning.[10]

In her Reith Lectures, Onora O'Neill has proposed a way to proceed: "Intelligent accountability, I suspect, requires more

[9] This rescuing literature (broadly available at any airport near you) is not very persuasive – with efforts to identify the attributes of leaders, and the ways such attributes can be acquired – but it goes through fascinating intellectual calisthenics to salvage this notion – e.g., *leadership without a leader*, etc. For an examination of the crucial differences between leadership and stewardship, see Gilles Paquet. 2009. "Stewardship versus Leadership" in G. Paquet, *Scheming virtuously – The road to collaborative governance*. Ottawa, ON: Invenire, chapter 5.

[10] Gilles Paquet. 2008. "A Plea for Intelligent Accountability," *Financial Management Institute Journal*, 19(2): 9-14; Michael E. Porter and Mark R. Kramer. 2011. "Creating Shared Value," *Harvard Business Review*, 89(1-2): 62-77.

attention to good governance and fewer fantasies about total control. Good governance is possible only if institutions are allowed some margin for self-governance of a form appropriate to their particular tasks, within a framework of financial and other reporting. Such reporting, I believe, is not improved by being wholly standardized or relentlessly detailed, and since much that has to be accounted for is not easily measured, it cannot be boiled down to a set of stock performance indicators. Those who are called to account should give an *account* of what they have done, and of their successes and failures, to others who have sufficient time and experience to assess the evidence and report on it."[11]

Recognizing (1) that the modern context is complex, and not easily reducible to simplistic cause-effect dyadic relationships, (2) that standardized measures of control are not effective, and may even generate, as toxic unintended consequences, a reduction in the level of trust, (3) that openness, transparency and quantophrenia may not be the unconditional goods that they are supposed to be, and (4) that it is absurd to pretend to manage our complex systems as if they were populated by either angelic Cartesian wantons or by a bunch of knaves and crooks – then what ensues is a new focus on *earned trust* in the long run, and much more attention, in the short run, to landmines like deception and misinformation.[12]

Instead of a sort of punitive accountability to hierarchical authorities, the new accountability is to partners and is geared to generating social learning. It aims at generating trust and collaboration, at reinforcing the moral contracts needed to

---

[11] O. O'Neill. 2002. *A Question of Trust*. Cambridge, UK: Cambridge University Press, p. 58.

[12] Experts like Paul Thomas have put more emphasis on trust building itself (P.G. Thomas. 2007. "Public Service of the 21st Century: Trust, Leadership, and Accountability," *www.optimumonline.ca*, 37(2): 19-24). The many ways in which one may build trust in the long term are quite important, but, in the short run, some focus on the major impediments to good governance is crucial. One needs to focus explicitly on some of the blockages, for the usual accountability apparatus would not appear to deal with major impediments like deception and misinformation.

facilitate social learning, at building on a refurbished notion of burden of office,[13] but mainly at stimulating *experimental accountability* – an accountability based on experience, and geared to increasing the probability of success.[14]

This is bound to transform the evaluation function completely: no longer a way to assert control, but a way to feed social learning and organizational development. The evaluator becomes a partner in the R&D of an organization and the architect of *developmental evaluation* – i.e., a value-adding process meant to contribute positively to whatever is being developed.[15]

Persiflage about the governance approach

The notion of governance has been under attack from a variety of perspectives in a variety of ways, not only by various potentates in the private, public and social sectors (for it was perceived as fundamentally questioning their legitimacy as leaders), but also by phalanxes of academics and practitioners who, having claimed exclusive competence on governing matters, have felt their monopolies expropriated by governance studies.

These attacks have suggested that governance is useless, ideologically-driven and toxic – and, when all this failed – reductive and Babelian tactics of encapsulation and sanitization of the notion of governance have been used.

Useless

The most common attack on governance is that leaders are in charge, and shared values exist – despite evidence to the contrary[16] – so that the present arrangements can be said

---

[13] Gilles Paquet. 1997. "The Burden of Office, Ethics and Connoisseurship," *Canadian Public Administration,* 40(1): 55-71.

[14] Charles F. Sabel. 2001. "A Quiet Revolution of Democratic Governance: Toward Democratic Experimentalism" in *Governance in the 21ˢᵗ Century.* Paris, FR: OECD, p. 121-148.

[15] Michael Quinn Patton. 2011. *Developmental Evaluation – Applying Complexity Concepts to Enhance Innovation and Use.* New York, NY: The Guilford Press.

[16] On the leadership front, see Harlan Cleveland. 2002. *Nobody in Charge.* San Francisco, CA: Jossey-Bass; on the shared values front, some recent Canadian

to work well and need not be repaired. The only problems that may materialize (if there are any) can therefore be cured by *management plumbing*. Minor adjustments to rules of conformance, better training of managers, stricter rules and tougher accountability enforcement, as well as more transparency, would eliminate whatever wrongs are purported to be ascribable to poor governance.

Retort

The documentation on pathologies of governance in all sectors makes pure denial less and less sustainable. As for the reliance on management plumbing repairs as panaceas, this is equally less and less persuasive when it is made clear that the central issue is not the minutiae of the principal-agent problem not being resolved, but the very notion of the agency being grossly misconceived.

What governance studies question is the foundational setting: the sanctity of the Westminster regime (in the public sector), of the shareholder-value dominance (in the private sector), and of the dominance of the permanent staff in the voluntary sector – all issues usually swept under the carpet by conventional wisdom – while peripheral anomalies are played up and addressed via stricter rules, more transparency and stricter enforcement. As a result, the governance flaws are simply occluded behind the reassuring verbiage of accountants, lawyers and the new training industry, which is focused entirely on propagandizing some protocols and etiquette of boards of directors. This entails nothing more than the best use of the *di Lampedusa principle* – to change everything (or seem to do so) in order that nothing changes.[17]

The only way to break down this denial attitude based on *learned blindness* is (1) to hammer away at the unrealistic nature of the assumptions on which the conventional Big 'G' is built,

---

survey data raise serious questions about them (Environics Institute. 2012. *The Common Good: who decides? – A National Survey of Canadians*. A Study commissioned by the Pierre Elliott Trudeau Foundation in collaboration with the University of Alberta, November 12).

[17] Immanuel Wallerstein. 1998. *Utopistics*. New York, NY: The New Press, p. 85.

on the omnipresence of governance pathologies,[18] on the costs of the governance failures, and on the futility of peripheral management plumbing; and (2) to multiply the examples of effective deconstruction of flawed governance processes with the help of the small 'g' *manière de voir,* and the demonstration of its ability to detect pathologies of coordination, to understand the source of governance mishaps, and to determine what might be suitable forms of repairs.

Ideological

When pure denial and the focus on plumbing do not work, governance is accused of being an ideological ploy by left and right wing squadrons. In the debates about governing, it is accused of neo-liberal sins by the left and of collectivist bias by the right.

Retort

In fact, governance is ideology-free. It simply claims that the social architecture of organizations has to be designed in keeping with a sound appreciation of the context within which they are meant to be nested and to operate. In that sense, the governance approach questions *all* the existing arrangements (old and new), and it does so continuously.

Private sector experts have been less immune to critical thinking as a result of both the massive changes in corporate governance through the creation of the European Union over the last 50 years,[19] and of the massive corporate scandals that could not be occluded in America. Public administration schools and practitioners have been more resistant to reasonable arguments because of their greater fundamentalism – rooted in their view of the sacred nature of the State, and of the clergy-like status of public sector workers.[20]

---

[18] Gilles Paquet. 2004. *Pathologies de gouvernance.* Montreal, QC: Liber.

[19] Gilles Paquet. 2008. *Gouvernance: mode d'emploi.* Montreal, QC: Liber, chapter 3.

[20] Ruth Hubbard and Gilles Paquet. 2010. *The Black Hole of Public Administration.* Ottawa, ON: The University of Ottawa Press.

To neutralize those ideological attacks, one has only to refer to Ross Ashby's law which established that a governing regime must be as complex as the organization or system it is trying to govern.[21]

Toxic

When the first two attacks fail, governance is damned because, by presuming that no one is in charge, the very crucial notions of accountability and responsibility are purported to be fundamentally undermined.

Retort

This is a groundless attack. The notion of 360-degree (or multiplex) accountability does not entail the demise of accountability but merely the disqualification of a certain notion of accountability. It does not exculpate guilty parties, but only recognizes that, in many instances, it would be abusive to declare personal or individual responsibility to be the dominant force, when such attribution cannot be defended given the circumstances. Responsibility often is not personal but structural. The propensity to invent a personalized guilty party at all costs – scapegoating – is indefensible.

Governance studies claim that traditional canons of conventional accountability appear to wish to salvage and rescue structures at all costs. When there is any question about flawed structures, panic strikes and 'accountabilism' kicks in – a mix of accountability and cannibalism – that suggests that it is sufficient to sacrifice and consume certain expiatory victims so that the structure can survive.[22] This is the situation that governance denounces. Responsibility and accountability must be adjudicated properly and not emotionally, and punishment must be imposed when appropriate, and not only on persons, but also on structures, when they are at fault.

---

[21] W. Ross Ashby. 1970. *An Introduction to Cybernetics*. London, UK: Chapman & Hall.

[22] David Weinberger. 2007. "The Folly of Accountabilism," *Harvard Business Review*, 85(2): 54.

The irresponsible defence of structures has led the traditional cosmology to surf insouciantly over quite murky situations where the new governance cosmology would have been much more exacting, and would have found flagrant evidence of lack of due diligence.[23] So it is wrong to presume that intelligent accountability (new style) is any less exacting than unintelligent accountability (old style).

Encapsulation and evanescence

The general failure of all those ill-inspired indictments – at the intellectual level – has not meant, however, that the governance point of view has prevailed. Another tactic has proved most effective in countering the surge of governance studies. Major actors like accountants, lawyers, academics and journalists have carried out a successful dual strategy of *encapsulation* of the notion of governance, and *sanitization/dilution* of its contents. Instead of facing head-on the broad perspective that challenged so many aspects of the paradigm in good currency,[24] they have embraced the subterfuge of reducing the notion of governance to fighting corruption (*à la* World Bank), tackling agency problems in the conventional framework, and catering to the mastery of some sort of etiquette of board management as the true nature of the governance challenge.[25]

Accountants, wedded to antiquarian scoreboards, have thereby completely avoided any critical thinking about unwarranted shareholder-value dominance, and concentrated mostly on debating the difficulties of ensuring the control of

---

[23] Ruth Hubbard and Gilles Paquet. 2007. *Gomery's Blinders and Canadian Federalism*. Ottawa, ON: The University of Ottawa Press, p. 48.

[24] For more details on the way these challenges can be tackled head-on, see Gilles Paquet and Tim Ragan. 2012. *Through the Detox Prism, op. cit.* (for corporate governance in the private sector); Ruth Hubbard and Gilles Paquet. 2010. *The Black Hole of Public Administration, op. cit.* (for governance in public administration); and Gilles Paquet. 2011. *Gouvernance collaborative: un antimanuel.* Montreal, QC: Liber, chapter 7 (for governance in the social sector).

[25] These sideshows amount to little more than re-arranging the chairs on the top deck of the Titanic.

managers by shareholders.[26] This has led to finessing control mechanisms of management at the very time when it had become clear that what was necessary was a rethinking of the whole co-governance process (actively involving other stakeholders and executives) that would mobilize the *affectio societatis* (commitment to engaged collaboration) and the knowledge and imagination of senior management.[27]

Lawyers have perfected the art of polishing the board composition and committee structure of boards of directors, and elaborating sophisticated rules of transparency and reporting at a time when the very substance of traditional corporate governance is in question, when new refurbished forms are being experimented with,[28] and major restructuring and refoundation of corporate governance are the order of the day.[29]

Academics and journalists have more subtly eviscerated the concept of its very substance by granting a chameleonesque quality to the notion of governance, such that it can be plastered on anything one chooses to apply it to. It is reminiscent of *Alice in Wonderland's* Humpty Dumpty's famous line: "When I use a word, it means just what I choose it to mean – neither more nor less." Such obfuscation can only undermine any meaningful multilogue on governance issues.

Some conjectures about the future of governance studies

There is no point in complaining about the blindness of the opposition to governance studies and its futility. In the face of

[26] Gilles Paquet. 2008. "Par quatre chemins plus ou moins subversifs" in G. Paquet, *Gouvernance : mode d'emploi*. Montreal, QC: Liber, p. 85-99.

[27] Vincent Cuisinier. 2008. *L'affectio societatis*. Paris, FR: Lexis-Nexis Litec; for a most ambitious reframing of this co-governance interface, see Blanche Segrestin and Armand Hatchuel. 2012. *Refonder l'entreprise*. Paris, FR: Seuil.

[28] See in particular the circumstances surrounding the emergence of the flexible purpose corporation in California (Gilles Paquet and Tim Ragan, 2012, *Through the Detox Prism, op.cit.*, chapter 4).

[29] Yvan Allaire and Mihaela Firsirotu. 2011. *A Capitalism of Owners*. Montreal, QC: IGOPP; Blanche Segrestin and Armand Hatchuel, 2012, *op.cit.*

any form of critical thinking, energized dynamic conservatism is to be expected from those whose position is assailed. The burden of proof always remains (and must remain) on the shoulders of those who are challenging conventional wisdom, and thereby undermining the *status quo*.

This daunting task has developed along four avenues in the case of the governance approach, and must proceed by:

- first, accumulating additional evidence of the pathologies generated by the arrangements proposed by the Big 'G' cosmology;
- second, developing clear and simple explanations of both the broad sources of these pathologies, and the generic ways in which better coordination can be restored;
- third, ensuring a good understanding of the limitations of what governance studies may deliver, so as not to generate unreasonable expectations; and
- fourth, helping to improve the awareness of the central importance of organizational design and design thinking in the budding new cosmology.

Exposing pathologies

Exposing pathologies serves as *revelateur* of governance failures, triggers the sort of inquiry into why they exist, and leads to the search for alternative arrangements likely to do better. Much work has been done on this front over the last few decades – both at the University of Ottawa's Centre on Governance and elsewhere. But until recently, this work has probably remained at too high a level of generality, too scattered in unlikely places of publication, and not sufficiently caustic.[30] It has allowed the defenders of the *status quo* to escape unscathed through the most superficial rhetoric, by taking advantage of the intellectual timidity of those attacking the *status quo*.

The Centre on Governance has been forceful on this front: exposing the weak underlying assumptions of the Big 'G' cosmology, and providing a variety of case studies of flagrant

---

[30] Excessive complacency and too much political correctness have often led to undue kindness and insufficient methodological cruelty in dealing with the persiflage directed at the governance approach.

governance failures in the public, private and social sectors. But future exposés should focus on particularly disastrous pathologies in the different issue domains and sectors, and be couched in sharper language if these criticisms are to break through the defence mechanisms in place. Nothing less will succeed in exorcizing the bunk anchored in decades of self-serving rationalizations.

But all of this will not suffice.

Alternative conceptual frameworks

One must also, in parallel, deconstruct more effectively the dynamics of these governance failures in a manner that explains how the harms have been generated, and how they might be attenuated. This can only come from a better understanding of the dual nature of the *rules of engagement* in the governance process: (1) the *incentive reward systems* at the foundation of the engagement of the different actors and members, but also (2) the *engagement mechanisms* at the core of the interaction order.

The first of these are at the core of the economics perspective, and have been probed extensively over the last few decades. The second of these are of a different nature, and emerge from a variety of systemic effects that depend much less on deliberate individual decisions than on *crowd phenomena* of all sorts (panic, contagion, synchronicity, etc.)[31] that have remained quite opaque, even though sociology has done considerable work on them.

A new composite tool box will need to be developed in which this second set of forces, in particular, will have to be better analyzed and harnessed if we are to probe the foundations of the blockages or contagious propulsive impacts that continue to appear somewhat difficult to understand. Unless these phenomena can be explicated and deconstructed, it is difficult to believe that alternative arrangements can be constructed, and avenues leading to required correctives fully explored.

---

[31] Marc Guillaume. 1989. *La contagion des passions*. Paris, FR: Plon; Jean-Pierre Dupuy. 2003. *La panique*. Paris, FR: Les Empêcheurs de penser en rond; Steven Strogatz. 2003. *Sync – The emerging science of spontaneous order*. New York, NY: Hyperion.

For example, different mechanisms at the core of this sort of dynamic have been examined by Mark Granovetter in his threshold models or studied by Laurent Thévenot in his probing of the dynamics of the regimes of engagement.[32]

In the first case, Granovetter has shown how thresholds of interaction (like conditions to join a movement) may trigger avalanches of support that are ascribable strictly to the mechanics of cumulative thresholds. This has been shown to be most important in explaining the dynamics of the Quebec student movement in the spring of 2012.[33]

In the second case, Thévenot has shown that, through the use of the dual nature of coordination (by competition in economics, and by way of trust in sociology), one may construct composite arrangements, building on their complementarity (e.g. incentive reward systems and moral contracts). This sort of accommodation between the instrumental rationality of the individual, and various social norms coming into play or not – depending on circumstances – can pragmatically generate various composite versions of effective engagement regimes.[34]

Learning to use such a new *outillage mental* underlines the difficulties and challenges generated by governance studies: having to transgress disciplinary barriers in developing new conceptual frameworks.

Limitations of governance

The Quantum quality of governance studies entails a degree of ambiguity that frustrates the quest for certainty.[35] It also

---

[32] Mark Granovetter. 1978. "Threshold Models of Collective Behavior," *American Journal of Sociology*, 83(6): 1,420-1,443; Laurent Thévenot. 2006. *L'action au pluriel – sociologie des régimes d'engagement*. Paris, FR: La Découverte.

[33] Gilles Paquet. 2012. "Deux hoquets de gouvernance: affaire Montfort et grogne étudiante québécoise en 2012," *www.optimumonline.ca*, 42(2): 32-60. This might also hold the key to the dynamics of the so-called Quebec "orange wave" in the 2012 Canadian federal election – a wave that brought the New Democratic Party to the status of loyal opposition in Canada's House of Commons.

[34] This is explored in Gilles Paquet and Tim Ragan, 2012, *Through the Detox Prism, op. cit.*, chapter 1.

[35] Gilles Paquet. 2012. "Gouvernance, science de l'imprécis," *Organisations & Territoires*, 21(3): 5-17.

ascribes such an importance to circumstances and contexts that scientific laws are most often beyond the governance expert's grasp. Indeed, a central feature of governance studies has been the recognition that discovering laws may be overly ambitious.

At best, it is perhaps only possible to work with mechanisms – processes that may or may not work, depending on the circumstances.[36] Recognizing that such is the case entails a shift away from the glorious search of *grand theories* toward *developing capacities to make good use of mechanisms* in the design of less inadequate forms of stewardship of organizations. This often means having to be satisfied with *bricolage* and nudging efforts through trial and error.

The difficulty is de-multiplied by the fuzziness of the vocabulary in use. Governance studies are plagued by the unspecialized language of suffering and the language of persuasion of advocacy that are in good currency. There is, as yet, no agreed upon language of problem solution in use. Most of the time, when the word governance is used, it is still in the most general sense of "how an organization or a system is run." Too often, this language is so vague that any commentary – even the most vacuous – may claim to be relevant. When compared with the highly stylized, congealed and crystallized vocabulary in the canons of management, public and social administration schools (however surreal and disconnected from reality they may be),[37] this creates a significant hurdle in the development of governance studies.

As a result, it may well be that, for the next while, the most bang for the buck will come from the demolition front. Establishing what will *not* work may appear unduly negative as a research program, but it may be the most important

[36] Jon Elster. 1989. *Nuts and Bolts for the Social Sciences.* Cambridge, UK: Cambridge University Press.

[37] For an illustration taken from public administration, see Ian Clark and Harry Swain. 2005. "Distinguishing the Real from the Surreal in Management Reform: Suggestions for Beleaguered Administrators in the Government of Canada," *Canadian Public Administration*, 48(4): 453-476.

contribution to make in the short run.[38] It is only when the conceptual frameworks have been further developed that greater ambitions should be entertained.

Design thinking

However, this oblique approach through the prevention of harm should not deter efforts to develop the new *outillage mental* to proceed ahead. Notions like stewardship, inquiring systems, developmental evaluations, etc. are already being increasingly used. But what is probably more important is the development of a *nouvel esprit* – a new frame of mind which leads to approaching organizations with a *design attitude*. It has already begun in the world of business,[39] but it has been much slower on other fronts, which are still at the stage where motivations are only beginning to be probed.[40]

Design cannot be reduced to problem-solving steps, fully programmable under a set of rules.[41] This is unduly reductive, since it assumes that the problem space (like an actual maze) has a structure that is already given. The design process does not really start with such givens. Schön defines it as the intelligent exploration of a terrain,[42] as an inquiry guided by an appreciative system carried over from history and past experience, that produces "a selective representation of an unfamiliar situation that sets values for the system's transformation. It frames the problem of the problematic situation, and thereby sets directions in which solutions lie, and provides a schema for exploring them."[43]

---

[38] One should not presume that this avenue is a blind alley, for harm-reduction through sabotaging processes generating harms is often quite efficient and effective. See Malcolm K. Sparrow. 2008. *The Character of Harms*. Cambridge, UK: Cambridge University Press.

[39] Roger Martin. 2009. *The Design of Business*. Boston, MA: Harvard Business Press.

[40] Julian Le Grand. 2003. *Motivation, Agency and Public Policy*. Oxford, UK: Oxford University Press.

[41] Donald A. Schön. 1990. "The Design Process" in V.A Howard (ed.). *Varieties of Thinking*. New York, NY: Routledge, p. 110-141.

[42] *Ibid.*, p. 125.

[43] *Ibid.*, p. 131-132.

Designing is a conversation with the situation that leads to experimenting with rules and guideposts that, in turn, reveals conflicts and dilemmas in the appreciative system. Since participants talk across discrepant frames, designing "is a process in which communication, political struggle, and substantive inquiry are combined ... [and it] may be judged appropriate ... if it leads to the creation of a design structure that directs inquiry toward progressively greater inclusion of features of the problematic situation and values for its transformation."[44] Such exploration leads to learning by doing, and "involves inquiry into systems that do not yet exist."[45] This will require a new attention to organizational design and to the theory and practice of social architecture.[46] This, in turn, requires a new way of thinking: *design thinking.*[47] This is a way of thinking that escapes groupthink and convergent thinking, which are designed to *make choices*, and favours divergent thinking, designed to *create choices*.

The focus of the inquiry in governance studies must shift from the *exploitation* of existing knowledge to *exploration* for new knowledge: a shift from routine management to the continuous reinvention of the organization, from a refining of arrangements in place, to exploration based as much on intuition as analysis, and a shift from short term and low risk to long term and high risk undertakings.[48]

---

[44] *Ibid.,* p. 138-139.

[45] A. George L. Romme. 2003. "Making a Difference: Organization as Design," *Organization Science,* 14(5): 558.

[46] Howard V. Perlmutter. 1965. *Towards a Theory and Practice of Social Architecture – The Building of Indispensable Institutions.* London, UK: Tavistock Publications.

[47] Tim Brown. 2009. *Change by Design.* New York, NY: Harper Business.

[48] James G. March. 1991. "Exploration and Exploitation in Organizational Learning," *Organization Science,* (2): 71-87; Roger Martin. 2009. *op. cit.,* p. 29.

This new way of thinking builds on experimentation, prototyping, and serious play,[49] and makes the highest and best use of grappling, grasping, discerning, and sense-making as part of reflective generative learning. It bypasses the simple use of focus groups, public engagement exercises and surveys as rearview mirrors into the future, because, as Tim Brown reminds us, Henry Ford used to say – if I'd asked my customers what they wanted, they'd have said 'a faster horse'.[50] Design thinking is a systematic approach to innovation: not being satisfied with managing existing offerings and adapting to new users, but creating new offerings for new users.[51]

Conclusion

Governance studies have emerged as a result of new realities demanding new schemes of interpretation. Over the past 20 years, they have confronted well-entrenched *problematiques* that have robustly resisted the invasion of this new paradigm. The conflict between the well-entrenched perspectives and the emergent ones has been a dubious battle: the traditional cosmologies have tried to immunize themselves from the subversion inspired by the governance approach, and to a great extent their rearguard action has succeeded. This is not surprising, since there is much resilient power in the sort of dynamic conservatism of those whose total intellectual capital is invested in the old ways. Yet the cost of the governance failures that are denied instead of repaired is becoming sufficiently large for many to be concerned.

[49] Prototyping means (1) identifying as quickly as possible some top requirements, (2) putting in place a quick-and-dirty provisional medium of co-development, (3) encouraging as many interested parties as possible to get involved as partners in designing a better arrangement, (4) encouraging iterative prototyping, and (5) thereby encouraging all, through playing with prototypes, to get a better understanding of the problems, of their priorities, and of themselves. (Gilles Paquet. 2009. *Crippling Epistemologies and Governance Failures – A Plea for Experimentalism*. Ottawa, ON: The University of Ottawa Press, p. 8; Michael Schrage. 2000. *Serious Play*. Boston, MA: Harvard Business School Press, 199ff).

[50] Tim Brown, 2009, *op.cit.*, p. 40.

[51] *Ibid.*, p. 161.

Some of the pillars of the old way of thinking (like top-down leadership) have been shaken. But the alternative governance *problematique* has not been fully worked out yet. So there are many on the sidelines who seem to be caught in a hiatus, in a state of transition: dissatisfied with the old scheme, but not entirely swayed by the new one – in part because of its unfinishedness, but also largely because of the new responsibilities governance bestows on the many who have grown satisfied with not being in charge at all.

Mythbusting has been only phase I: much of the work up to now has shown that Big 'G' does not work, and that small 'g' collaborative governance is not unworkable. Phase II is an invitation to sabotage the harms uncovered through the phase I inquiries. It is not as good and promising as a road map, but it is bound to help clear the road ahead ... perhaps sufficiently that some will be tempted to proceed immediately to phase III – to explore new possibilities – the design thinking phase.

| Wicked Problems and Social Learning

"We hunger for certainty. That is a big problem.
It might even be THE problem."

Adam Frank

Introduction

The social sciences, in general, have taken a positivist turn over the last century. They have come to present society and organizations as a given set of more or less mechanical and predictable objects that can be understood through experimental investigation and observation. Indeed, such a process has come to be regarded as the only avenue capable of generating substantial and credible knowledge. Yet this approach is too simplistic to provide useful representations of our multiplex and turbulent world. Consequently, dogmas have led social scientists to contort the questions they probe to ensure that they comply with the requirements of simplistic conventional positivist science. This has meant that unrealistic assumptions have flourished and become conventional, and that the fundamental concerns that did not fit this truncated perspective have been banished to the land of non-studies.

Moreover, the evidence-based mantra used to suggest that differences of opinion (if any) can be resolved by the arbitration of the scientific method is itself highly questionable. When many legitimate viewpoints exist, and a variety of dimensions

– economic, social, political, cultural, moral, etc. – are of import, the very notion of "goals" is unclear, and means-ends relationships are also unreliable. We are beyond concerns of optimization and consistency, but also beyond the powers of arbitration of science; we are in the world of *wicked problems* and in the republic of *trans-science*, where policy problems cannot be resolved by the scientific method.[1]

The governance perspective responds to wicked problems in a trans-scientific way. It is in the business of inquiring about the nature of the problem at the source of the discomfort, of enabling collaboration among those potential partners who have a portion of the power, the resources and the information (despite their different values), and of designing and constructing modes of *stewardship* that do not yet exist, but are *ecologically rational* – i.e., matching strategy and environment (in the broadest sense of the terms). This approach aims at creating a wholly new and unprecedented situation, a new reality and a new knowledge. It builds on *social learning*.[2]

The first section of this chapter outlines, in a most general way, the sub-processes that make up the particular brand of this social learning approach that has been developed over the last few decades at the Centre on Governance. The second section fleshes out the substance of the components of the social learning approach (including the development of *negative capability* – the capacity to keep going and collaborating when things are going wrong), and it identifies some important enabling contextual resources. The third section focuses on the centrality of design thinking and presents a skeletal roadmap in the design of collaborative governance. The fourth section explains why a change in attitude and vocabulary – *from a focus*

[1] For the notion of wicked problems, see Horst W.J. Rittel and Melvin M. Webber. 1973. "Dilemmas in a General Theory of Planning," *Policy Sciences,* (4): 155-169; for the notion of trans-science, see Alvin M. Weinberg. 1974. "Science and Trans-Science," *Minerva,* 10(2): 209-222.
[2] John Friedmann and George Abonyi. 1976. "Social Learning: A Model for Policy Research," *Environment & Planning,* A(8), 927-940; Gilles Paquet. 1999. "Tackling Wicked Problems" in G. Paquet. *Governance Through Social Learning.* Ottawa, ON: The University of Ottawa Press, p. 41-52.

on decision (on the assumption that the problem is already defined and the information available) *to a focus on design* (on the assumption that the problem definition has to be constructed, and a wholly new unprecedented situation has to be created) – is foundational, and how it can be operationalized. In closing, we reflect on the means to manage the transition to this new attitude and new vocabulary.

Even though this approach may appear to some as being somewhat imprecise, imprecision does not reflect a lack of rigour.[3]

The social learning response to the wicked problems challenge

To deal with wicked problems, analysts must learn on the job about both the configuration of facts and values defining the issues. They must also learn from the stakeholders, as well as from the megacommunity, for without their participation (active and passive) it is unlikely that a collaborative governance apparatus can be distilled that will synthesize, reconcile and transcend the perspectives of the different potential partners. Neither can an effective and sustained collaboration be generated among those who hold a portion of the power, resources and information required to ensure effective wayfinding, resilience and innovation.

A broad gauging of the corridor of possibilities

Some decades ago, Friedmann and Abonyi stylized a simple *social learning exploratory model of policy research* to deal with wicked problems. They have suggested that it requires responding to four questions about any possible action plan: Is it technically feasible? Is it socially acceptable? Is it too politically destabilizing? Is it implementable? In order to respond to these questions, one requires some appreciation (1) of appropriate theories of reality, (2) of the ways social values are expressed, (3) of the political game within which the design exercise is carried out, and (4) of the ways in which collective action is carried out.

---

[3] Gilles Paquet. 2012. "La gouvernance, science de l'imprécis," *Organisations & Territoires*, 21(3): 5-17.

These four pillars of social learning are interconnected, and any change in one affects the others. This paradigm of social practice in policy research is synthesized in Figure 1.

FIGURE 1

A Social Learning Model of Policy Research

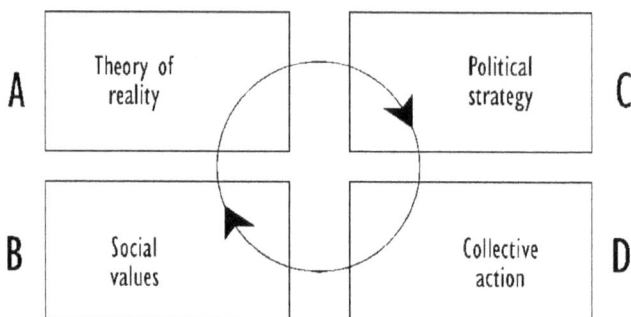

Source: Friedman and Abonyi, 1976, op. cit., p. 88.

Block B in Figure 1 is the locus of the nexus of the different values systems that provide normative guidance, either in the transformation of reality or in the selection of strategies for action. Theory of reality (Block A) refers to a symbolic representation and explanation of the complex environment. Political strategy (Block C) connotes the political game which generates the course of action chosen. Collective action (Block D) deals with implementation and the interaction with partner groups. Together, these four components come to life in concrete situations.

Traditional approaches to policy research focus on attempts to falsify hypotheses about some objective reality, according to the canons of scientific experimentation. This is too narrow a focus for policy research when the ground is in motion. For the *social practitioner*, what is central is an effort "to create a wholly new, unprecedented situation that, in its possibility for generating new knowledge, goes substantially beyond the initial hypothesis." The social learning paradigm is built on reflection-in-action, dialogue and mutual learning by experts and clients: i.e., on an interactive or trans-active style of planning. "The paradigm makes the important epistemological assumption that action hypotheses are verified as 'correct' knowledge only in the course of a social practice that includes the four components of theory (of reality), the configuration of values, strategy and action. A further epistemological commitment is to the creation of a new reality, and hence to a new knowledge, rather than in establishing the truth-value of propositions in abstraction from the social context to which they are applied."[4] Similar general ideas have been explored over time by many others, including Carl Taylor.[5]

This social learning framework has been used most effectively in analyzing phenomena like multiculturalism.[6] But this formulation of the social learning approach has not been sufficiently well operationalized, from the start, to foster wide adoption and extensive applications of this approach to the large number of wicked problems in need of such an approach. What has been missing is a more carefully spelled out version of this approach in stages – not in order that it be applied mechanically and thoughtlessly, but in order to make it more easily useable as a reference protocol for analysts interested in applying it to various issue domains.

The contours of the Centre on Governance's version of social learning
The social learning approach, as practiced at the Centre on Governance, is based on the assumptions that:

1. One does not usually have *ab ovo* a good grasp of the situation; consequently, collaborative governance requires one to start with a process of inquiry to ascertain the state of affairs, and to gather the necessary information that is spread widely among stakeholders and potential partners.

[4] John Friedmann and George Abonyi 1976. *op.cit.*, p. 938; Donald A. Schön. 1983. *The Reflective Practitioner.* New York, NY: Basic Books.
[5] Carl A. Taylor. 1997. "The ACIDD Test: a framework for policy planning and decision-making," *Optimum*, 27(4): 53-62.
[6] Gilles Paquet. 2008. *Deep Cultural Diversity – A Governance Challenge.* Ottawa, ON: The University of Ottawa Press.

2. Most potential partners have no shared values or common purposes, and no one has all the information, resources and power to fully take charge and to guide the organization in ways assuring resilience and innovation, so what must be constructed are arenas or symbolic platforms where these diverse perspectives can be blended into a more or less viable evolving syncretic perspective.

3. The inquiring system and the blending of perspectives may be *necessary* to elicit a mix of principles, conventions, rules and mechanisms to ensure effective coordination and to construct the equivalent of an automatic pilot to generate wayfinding, resilience and innovativeness, but they are *not sufficient* conditions. The infrastructure of social learning must be in place to feed the exploration and the probing through the detection and correction of incongruities as the organization proceeds through the social learning cycle.

4. It is naïve to pretend that collaborative governance emerging in this manner will necessarily be able to resist and survive in the face of failure and tough times. It will be essential to ensure the development of *negative capability* (in the sense of John Keats): the capability to keep going when things are going wrong, through the operations of fail-safe and safe-fail mechanisms, and other ways of sustaining commitment.

This approach is meant to immunize the inquiring system against the false sense of virtue in decisiveness that leads so many to take action prematurely, and with undue haste, before a good grasp of the situation is gained. Not only is this undue haste likely to be both myopic, and not to embrace the full range of possibilities, but it is also likely to sabotage the nurturing and maintaining of the commitment of partners by falling prey to the *urgence de conclure*.

The engine of social learning and wayfinding

Whatever stewardship emerges is not entirely the result of a deliberate strategy, but is in the nature of *emerging wayfinding*, as a result of a variety of gestures and actions by partners (as the experience unfolds), with the result that additional knowledge accrues and triggers yet more gestures and actions. Policy and strategy are not mainly about managing resources to some advantage, as gauged by an objective function (even though it has been reduced to this by managers as a matter of convenience), but about "attaining and sustaining a set of organized relationships nested within wider systems in order to experience the possibility of doing things differently and, potentially, better."[7]

What may not be obvious from such a depiction is the extent to which, in a small 'g' governance world, engagement with the environment and the partners entails "local adaptations and ingenuity in everyday practical coping ... acting with purpose to deal with immediate concerns at hand but doing so in habituated ways ... ."[8] Wayfinding means "reaching out into the unknown and developing an incomplete but practically sufficient comprehension of the situation in order to cope effectively with it. Prospective rather than retrospective sense-making is involved ... (and wayfinding) is continuously clarified through each iterative action and adjustment, and not through any predetermined agenda."[9]

Social learning a: cognition and information diffusion

An inquiring system has no safe and assured pathway ahead. It is a proactive probing and exploration system that is on the lookout for anomalies, their sources and causes, for cumulatively clarified problem definitions, for the identification of who needs to be involved in dealing with the issue, for ways in

---

[7] Robert C.H. Chia and Robin Holt. 2009. *Strategy Without Design – The Silent Efficacy of Indirect Action.* Cambridge, UK: Cambridge University Press, p. ix, 112.

[8] *Ibid.*, p. 159.

[9] *Ibid.*, p. 159.

which micro-reactions might be cast in more general contexts, for groping instruments as well as for alliances and moral contracts with other parties that might help in the process and, finally, for anything that might help in accelerating the process of social learning and experimentation, and in opening new vistas. The success of the operation should be gauged not so much by reference to myopic measurable temporary outcomes (that may often be quite misleading), but mainly by the modification of habituations and belief systems, and by the effectiveness of the mechanisms in place to modify the very nature of the game, if and when the inquiring system gives signs of being derailed or of being guided out of the corridor defined by acceptable norms.[10]

In an effort to help identify the major obstacles to social learning, Max Boisot has suggested a simple mapping of the social learning cycle in a three-dimensional space – *the information space* – which maps the degree of *abstraction*, *codification* and *diffusion* of the information flows within organizations. The farther away from the origin on the vertical axis, the more the information is codified (i.e., the more its form is clarified, stylized and simplified); the farther away from the origin laterally eastward, the more widely the information is diffused and shared; and the farther away from the origin laterally westward, the more abstract the information is (i.e., the more general the categories in use).

The social learning cycle in Figure 2 can be decomposed into two phases, with three steps in each phase: Phase I emphasizes the cognitive dimensions of the cycle; Phase II, the diffusion of the new information.

---

[10] Max H. Boisot. 1995. *Information Space*. London, UK: Routledge; Gilles Paquet. 2009. *Scheming virtuously – The road to collaborative governance*. Ottawa, ON: Invenire, chapter 5.

FIGURE 2
Learning Cycle and Potential Blockages

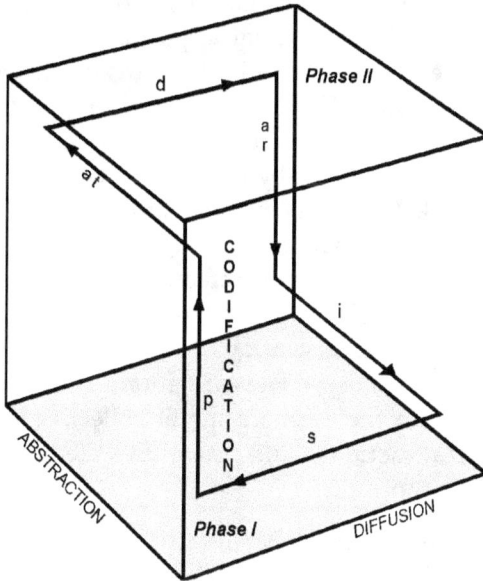

In Phase I, learning begins with some scanning of the environment in order to detect anomalies and paradoxes. Following this first step (s), one is led in step 2 to stylize the problem (p), posed by the anomalies and paradoxes, in a language of the problem solution; the third step of Phase I purports to generalize the solution found to the more specific issue to a broader family of problems through a process of abstraction (at). In Phase II, the new knowledge is diffused (d) to a larger community of persons or groups in step 4; then there is a process of absorption (ar) of this new knowledge by the population, so as to become part of the tacit stock of knowledge in step 5; and in step 6, the new knowledge is not only absorbed, but has an impact (i) on the concrete practices of the group or community.

Figure 2 enables us to identify the different potential blockages through the learning cycle. In Phase I, cognitive dissonance in (s) may prevent the anomalies from being noted; inhibitions of all sorts in (p) may stop the process of translation into a language of problem solution; and blockages (at) may keep the new knowledge from acquiring the most effective degree of generality. In Phase II, the new knowledge may not get the appropriate diffusion because of property rights (d), or because of the strong dynamic conservatism, which may generate a refusal to listen by those most likely to profit from the new knowledge (ar), or because of difficulties in finding ways to incorporate the new knowledge (i).

Figure 2 may be interpreted as making possible a checklist of potential sources of blockages or failures in the inquiring system. Interventions to remove or to attenuate the learning blockages always entail some degree of interference with the mechanisms of collective intelligence, relational transactions, and therefore the psycho-social fabric of the organization.

Social learning β: collaboration

A crucial component of this inquiring system is collaboration. For if power, resources and information are widely distributed among many hands and heads, no effective wayfinding can emerge without collaboration. Yet participants are different; they are invited to stay connected and to engage with persons with different belief systems. This cannot be accomplished without some modicum of trust, sharing, belonging and respect in this co-creation process, even though the only truly shared sentiment to begin with is discomfort with the *status quo*.[11]

Collaboration means recognizing that one cannot do it alone, that one must take a step beyond individual needs "to call forth possibilities from an unknown and not-yet-possible future." Such a courage to collaborate translates into a way of being. This will be instituted in a variety of conventions: some explicit and legal, others tacit and quasi-emotional.

---

[11] Alycia Lee and Tatiana Glad. 2011. *Collaboration: the courage to step into a meaningful mess.* Provo, UT: Berkana Institute.

Collaboration is meant to broaden the problem definition and to widen the potential responses to problems that emerge from silo-thinking, but it is never clear that these possibilities will materialize. It requires the capacity to keep going, and to endure when things look not too promising, but also the capacity to change course when the original arrangement proves ineffective. As Chia and Holt would put it, the right balance would be the freedom "from both the obstinacy of the commonplace and the iridescent glare of the new."[12]

The ecology of the inquiring system at work entails a cycle of social learning in four phases (Table 2) that might be regarded as the standard learning process in normal times – with *an observation/cognitive phase, an investigative phase, a design-cum-moral contracts phase,* and *an evaluative and social learning phase.*

Since most policies are likely to fail, the inquiring system has to be equipped with the requisite mechanisms to ensure that the system can minimize the costs of failure: routine *fail-safe mechanisms* (FSM) aimed at ensuring *resilience,* i.e., keeping the organization within a corridor constrained by certain bounds in normal times.

Table 2 Provisional Checklist of Questions

I Does the situation need changing?	II What is the problem?	III How will you work together?	IV How will you learn together & evaluate your progress?
1. Are there any detectable anomalies?	6. What is the task at hand?	a. DESIGN	12. What feedback & informational loops do you have to enable social learning?
2. What are the salient features of the issue domain?	7. What are the non-negotiable constraints within the mega-community?	10. What instruments of collaboration and social learning can you use to produce short-term success and long-term commitment?	13. What collective learning processes do you have in place?
3. What are the causal mechanisms at play?	8. Who are the stakeholders that must be included and how will you involve them?	b. CONVENTIONS	14. How will you gauge ongoing performance objectively?
4. Can this be resolved by a single actor?	9. What are the risks and potential rewards, and how will these be aligned among the various partners?	11. What are the conventions & moral contracts that need to be negotiated to maintain a culture of collaboration?	15. How will you gauge changes in attitudes & behaviours among partners?
5. Who are the key stakeholders?			16. How will you resolve conflicts?
			17. What safe-fail mechanisms are in place?
			18. At what point would you dissolve the collaboration?

Source: Gilles Paquet and Christopher Wilson. 2011. "Collaborative Co-governance as Inquiring Systems," www.optimumonline.ca, 41(2): 1-12.

Social learning γ: dynamic re-organizational level

Organizations and systems are also periodically hit by shocks that threaten the very existence of the original setting. A set of essential variables is affected, and it triggers step-mechanisms that command fundamental transformations if the system is to survive. *Safe-fail mechanisms* (SFM) are meant to trigger *effective renewal* when the organization is faced with dramatic forms of creative destruction, experiences that command self-transformation and self-reinvention as the only way to survive.

Buzz Holling and other experts have suggested that both natural and human organizations go through somewhat periodic eco-cycles of the sort sketched in Figure 3.

FIGURE 3
The Organizational Eco-cycle

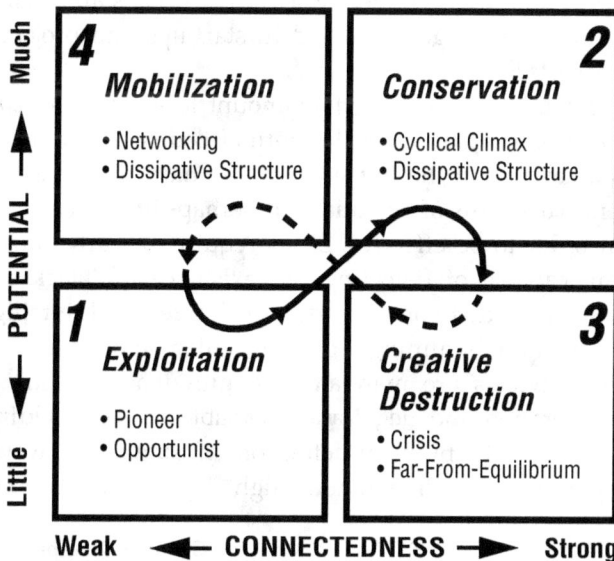

Adapted from C.S. (Buzz) Holling. 1987. "Simplifying the Complex: The paradigms of ecological function and structure," European Journal of Operational Research, (30): 139-146; and David K. Hurst and Brenda J. Zimmerman. 1994. "From Life Cycle to Ecocycle: A New Perspective on the Growth, Maturity, Destruction and Renewal of Complex Systems," Journal of Management Inquiry, 3(4): 349.

According to this view, organizations move from situations of exploitation of existing resources (Phase 1 – low potential, loose connectedness, entrepreneurial), to moments when more tightly connected forms of organization (institutionalized and more strongly connected in order to fully take advantage of a higher potential) bump into constraints due to the very rigidities brought forth by institutionalization (Phase 2 – bureaucratization, rigidity). This leads to vulnerability to changes that can be a threat to inflexible organizations, facing Schumpeterian shocks and crises created by innovations as a result of environmental pressures or technical breakthroughs (Phase 3 – crisis, fragmentation). Then, either the organization cannot cope (with the result that it disappears or is dramatically wounded), or it reacts by a renewal that mobilizes resources in new configurations, often much more loosely connected, as a result of creative tension (Phase 4 – diverse paths to renewal, high potential, weak connectedness). The cycle starts again as this new potential gets diffused in start-ups and projects of diverse sorts.[13]

SFMs create something tantamount to a *state of exception* that temporarily suspends the normal course of affairs, and plays a key role in the transition from Phase 3 to Phase 4, to prevent crucial loss of potential and perhaps implosion.

In order to be effective, SFMs require an early warning system, capable of detecting the existence of 'black swan phenomena': either some *observatory* charged with intelligent environmental scanning, or particular moments when mission reviews are mandated. Required as well are *fora* for deliberation and negotiation, capable of (1) providing a refinement of the problem definition; (2) suggesting ways in which improved collaboration might be generated; and (3)

---

[13] C.S. (Buzz) Holling. 1987. "Simplifying the Complex: The paradigms of ecological function and structure," *European Journal of Operational Research*, (30): 139-146; David K. Hurst and Brenda J. Zimmerman. 1994. "From Life Cycle to Ecocycle: A New Perspective on the Growth, Maturity, Destruction and Renewal of Complex Systems," *Journal of Management Inquiry*, 3(4): 339-354.

proposing mechanisms through which newly discovered impediments to such collaboration might be neutralized. Finally, there must be a real possibility of *experimentation* on the road to renewal in full awareness of the tentative nature of the experiments.[14]

Such mechanisms need not necessarily result in explicit, drastic, or glorious revolutions. Often, in environments crippled by a culture of entitlements and powerful mental prisons, draconian moves can only lead to confrontations from which little can emerge but stalemates. As a result, much change occurs underground, *petit à petit*, with as little controversial public discussion as possible, but not necessarily in a less effective way – to the despair of those obsessed by the need for explicit deliberation theatrics.

Social learning δ: reflexive governance and negative capability

Sequentially

If one had to stylize the stewardship process through social learning in a sequential way, one might make use of the template used by practitioners.[15]

Stage A begins with some perceived gap between current reality and some desirable outcome as a trigger to direct attention toward initiating action. This originates with the recognition that action is required (either individually or collectively), and the subsequent exploration of action possibilities.

Stage B is a concurrent search for the mobilization of required partners and the nurturing of the necessary collaboration. This dual and interactive sub-process calls for:

[14] A general approach has been sketched in Ruth Hubbard and Gilles Paquet. 2006. "Réinventer notre architecture institutionnelle," *Policy Options*, 27(7): 57-64; Joseph McCann, John Selsky and James Lee. 2009. "Building Agility, Resilience and Performance in Turbulent Environments, *People & Strategy*, 32(3): 44-51.

[15] John Parr et al. 2002. *The Practice of Stewardship*. Mountain View, CA: Alliance for Regional Stewardship.

Mobilization	Collaboration
• the correct framing of critical issues and opportunities and focusing attention on what needs to be done	• the creation of platforms for people to work together
• the communication of key information likely to inspire, rally and motivate a broader set of people to take part in the diverse networks	• the development of new relationships capable of generating tangible results and thereby of changing mindsets, and encouraging creative thinking

Stage C has to do with efforts to sustain change through creating and renewing institutions, and re-igniting the process by refocusing on new challenges and opportunities. This entails much conceptual refurbishment and efforts to agitate and rekindle the social learning process through reframing the very notion of what is possible.

What is required is a capacity for the organization to learn, i.e., to reflect on its own experience, to make sense of it and to retool, restructure, and even to reframe the basic questions facing the organization in order to generate effective ways to discern and grapple with the generative challenge of learning. These requirements have been spelled out by practitioners of *reflexive governance*. They may be summarized as follows: knowledge integration and learning by doing; capacity for long-run anticipation of systemic effects; adaptivity of strategies and institutions; iterative experimental and participatory definition of broad directions; and interactive strategy development.[16]

But there is also a need to develop *negative capability* – capability to continue to collaborate when the going is tough and disappointing. This sort of commitment may be rooted in *affectio societatis* at first, but this will not suffice: it must be nurtured.

Instrumentally: competencies and affordances
Since dynamic adaptation is the core process, such stewardship action requires competencies that need to be

---

[16] Wilfred H. Drath and Charles J. Palus. 1994. *Making Common Sense.* Greensboro, NC: Center for Creative Leadership; Jan-Peter Voβ. et al. (eds.). 2006. *Reflexive Governance for Sustainable Development.* Cheltenham, UK: Edward Elgar.

nudged into existence, not only by leveraging the existing forces of self-organization, but also by harnessing them somewhat.

These required competencies may be divided into five categories:[17]

1. contextual (embrace uncertainty and error, building bridges, reframing, improvise, adapt, overcome);
2. interpersonal (consultation, negotiation, deliberation, conflict resolution, facilitation, brokering, preceptoring, educating, animating, changing roles);
3. enactment (enabling, empowering, responsiveness, creativity);
4. systems values (ethics of interconnectiveness and interdependence, removing obstacles, freeing others to act better);
5. staying the course while rocking the boat (imagination, experimentation, responsibility to explore, emphasis on sins of omission, learning by prototyping).

These capacities are not only individual, but collective, in the sense that rules of interaction among individuals generate emerging properties that derive from the dynamics of situations, not only from the heads of actors. The interaction order (in the language of Goffman) generates a sort of collective intelligence, a sort of social mind.[18]

The dual (individual and collective) capacities are obviously interacting and confronted with a context that affords 'action possibilities' but not others. Affordances are indicators of potentialities and possibilities – like a door knob for turning, a plate for pushing, etc. *Affordances are invitations to certain uses.* Whether these affordances are real or perceived is of less relevance than the fact that they open and limit the realm of possibilities. In particular, the context generates affordances

[17] Donald N. Michael. 1993. "Governing by Learning: Boundaries, Myths, and Metaphors," *Futures*, 25(1): 81-89; Jonathan Hughes and Jeff Weiss. 2007. "Simple Rules for Making Alliances Work," *Harvard Business Review*, 85(11): 122-131.

[18] Erving Goffman. 1959. *The Presentation of Self in Everyday Life*. Garden City, NY: Doubleday; Howard Rheingold. 2002. *Smart Mobs*. Cambridge, UK: Perseus.

that individuals and collectivities perceive or learn to perceive. Learning to perceive affordances is a key kind of perceptual learning.[19] "Affordances are … relationships that hold between objects and agents … to discover and make use of affordances is one of the important ways" to deal with novel situations.[20]

Learning to perceive affordances better, or developing ways to improve such perception is the substance of social learning, and is at the core of innovation and innovative design. This is the way in which the automatic pilot is improved.

Contextually: megacommunity, common knowledge, synchronization

The dynamic of stewardship focuses on information and communication. But it need not be, as mentioned earlier, only through the head of actors: it may equally emerge from context and situations. All the dimensions explored earlier are important (components, guideposts, process, framework, competencies, affordances), but they remain incomplete unless some *enabling resources* can be added – like the megacommunity, common knowledge and the forces of synchronization – that are at the core of self-organization and constitute the sort of glue that makes these other components hang together.

This is not the place to probe these matters at great length, but they cannot be ignored altogether.

Megacommunity

A megacommunity – i.e., "a public sphere in which organizations and people deliberately join together around a compelling issue of mutual importance, following a set of practices and principles that will make it easier to achieve results"[21] – entails a requisite amount of both trust (institutional, inter-organizational, and interpersonal) and social capital.

---

[19] Donald A. Norman. 1999. "Affordances, Conventions and Design," *Interactions,* 6(3): 38-43.

[20] Donald A. Norman. 2007. *The Design of Future Things.* New York, NY: Basic Books, p. 68-69.

[21] Mark Gerencser et al. 2006. "The Mega-Community Manifesto," *www. strategy-business.com,* August 16.

Gerencser et al. have identified four critical elements for a thriving megacommunity: (1) understanding the problems to be resolved, the necessary players and partners, and the ways in which they affect one another; (2) the presence of partners in a listening, learning and understanding mode; (3) the designing and customizing of suitable cross-sector arrangements; and (4) experiments: learning from them, and effective collective monitoring of progress accomplished by the megacomunity.

People and groups potentially affected by or involved in stewardship are, by definition, players in the megacommunity. For all of them, their interests in it (and views of it) will tend to be framed by the mindset that dominates the culture in good currency in the socio-economic context. Their opinions will evolve to some extent as time passes, and will change to a greater or lesser degree as a result of external influences.

Common knowledge

Another set of forces that is most important in the dynamics of stewardship is common knowledge. Chwe has shown that "coordination is often achieved through adaptation and evolution and implicit communication, but people often explicitly communicate"[22] in order to solve them. He shows, looking at how common knowledge emerges, that it is often through communicative events like rituals, ceremonies and other cultural practices. He demonstrates how the problem of indeterminacy in coordination can be resolved by common knowledge through rituals. It indicates ways in which intervention might nudge people toward coordination through generating common knowledge, and allowing choices to be made by actors on that basis (i.e., allowing self-organization to proceed).

This approach explicitly leverages the cultural and informational contexts likely to generate effective self-organization.

---

[22] Michael S.Y. Chwe. 2001. *Rational Ritual*. Princeton, NJ: Princeton University Press, p. 98-99.

Synchronization

Yet another set of forces at work in the dynamics of stewardship has to do with synchronization: the fact that, for reasons that are not always clear, humans, like animals, would appear to fall into synchronized behaviour in self-organized ways (traffic flows, applause, etc.). Strogatz has thoroughly reviewed the existence of synchronization in the animal and human worlds: the spontaneous outbreak of coordinated or herd or mob behaviour, with certain thresholds (or mix of thresholds for different groups), defining tipping points where mass synchronization occurs.[23]

Strogatz has shown that, in the animal world, spontaneous coordination is omnipresent (fireflies flashing in unison, flocks of birds flying in formation, etc.). It has also been shown that synchronization occurs in the material world of lifeless things like clocks. In the human world, group think, coordination of menstrual cycles, etc., are also well documented. In the same way, synchronization materializes in group behaviour, and we are beginning to understand the mechanisms underlying such generation of order out of chaos when certain thresholds are reached. This illustrates in a simple way the forces of self-organization that need to be taken into account.

Such forces of synchronization need not generate orderly coordination. They often generate heart fibrillation or mobs. But understanding such forces is fundamental if there is any hope of finding the equivalent of a defibrillator at the social level.

The dynamics of stewardship underpinning the metaphor of the automatic pilot need to be understood as a nexus of mechanisms, many of which are designed with certain purposes in mind, but many others of which are simply the result of self-organization, either triggered by common knowledge, or as unintended consequences of context, situations and experimental interventions, or as a result of sync.

While this definition of stewardship does not promise the simplicity guaranteed in the literature on imperial leadership,

---

[23] Steven Strogatz. 2003. *Sync – The Emerging Science of Spontaneous Order.* New York, NY: Hyperion.

it has the advantage of defining a program of research that is immensely more promising and realistic. It escapes from the simplistic anthropomorphic images of governing, by recognizing both the full extent to which mechanisms can be put in place capable of nudging the organization in preferred directions, as well as the full extent to which experiments with prototypes to tinker with complex non-linear systems are likely to generate important unintended consequences as a result of the self-organization they trigger. Such an approach may not always promise success in governing organizations, but it provides an insight into the ways in which governing might succeed through a mix of the good use of context and design thinking.

Scoping design thinking

In 2004, Karl Weick published a paper in which he rooted his reflections on rethinking organizational design in the examination of the testimonies of two well-known designers: Frank Gehry (the famous architect) and Dee Hock (the ex-CEO who designed VISA)[24] – both blessed with an uncanny ability at such work. The main lesson Weick drew from these reflections is that even though coordination is a central concern of designers – the job of generating contraptions that not only reconcile the pressures from the geo-technical constraints and from the values and plans of the various stakeholders, through coordinating the activities of all those who have a significant portion of the information, resources and power that need to be mobilized to ensure resilience and innovation – there is a danger that allowing a fixation on some rigid and impatient coordination imperative might impair the whole process of design.

[24] Karl E. Weick. 2004. "Rethinking Organizational Design" in Richard J. Boland and Fred Collopy (eds.). *Managing by Design*. Stanford, CA: Stanford University Press, p. 36-53. He used Frank Gehry. 1999. "Commentaries" in M. Friedman (ed.). *Architecture + process: Gehry talks*. New York, NY: Rizzoli, p. 43-287, and Dee Hock. 1999. *Birth of the Chaordic Age*. San Francisco, CA: Berrett-Koehler.

Weick quotes Dee Hock as observing that management is unduly focused on creating "constants, uniformity and efficiency", when what is required in our turbulent world is to understand and coordinate "variability, complexity and effectiveness." Weick suggests that these modern requirements identified by Hock "are best achieved if design is recast as designing that uses transient constructs, *bricolage*, and improvisation."[25]

This emphasis on on-going and living processes has a Deweyian flavour: John Dewey always refused to use terms with static connotation, like thing or object, to connote human realities and activities. He preferred using the elusive notion of *affairs*. In the words of a Dewey scholar, "affairs are never frozen, finished or complete. They form a world characterized by genuine contingency and continual process. A world of affairs is a world of actualities open to a variety of possibilities."[26]

Therefore, for Weick and others, *one must design for transience and incompleteness*: being satisfied to define the skeleton or bare bones framework and to allow an emergent structure to develop around it as partners interact, argue, come together, and learn along the way. This is exactly what Gehry and Hock would appear to have been doing, and this is the spirit that informs a skeletal roadmap for design in three stages and nine steps:

STAGE 1
a) **New attitude and vocabulary**
b) **Inquiring system:** epistemology
c) **Mental mapping:** some ethnography

STAGE 2
a) **Thinking with our hands**: a bit of process thinking *à la* Friedmann and Abonyi
b) **Collaboration**
c) **Prototyping and serious play**: about reframing, restructuring, retooling

---

[25] Weick, 2004, *op.cit.*, p. 47.

[26] Raymond D. Boisvert. 1998. *John Dewey – Rethinking Our Time*. Albany, NY: State University of New York Press, p. 24 (quoted by R. Garud, S. Jain and P. Tuertscher. 2008. "Incomplete Design and Designing Incompleteness," *Organization Studies*, (29): 351-371).

STAGE 3

a) Social learning: gauging according to various metrics

b) Engagement and storytelling: moral contracts + learning loops

c) Etiquette and ethics of prototyping: corridor phenomena

These stages are not a list of mechanical steps that must be followed *seriatim* in a servile manner. The sequence is rather analogous to working through a number of transparencies (used in yesteryear with an overhead projector) that sequentially introduce families of concerns that are overlaid, one upon the other, to represent cumulatively (and through an ever more sophisticated and higher-definition image of complex natural or social systems) a mix of different intermingled sub-systems, making up the whole organization or social system. For instance, in elementary school one would start with the skeleton of a human body and overlay on it the muscular system, the nervous system, etc.

This analogy with transparency overlays is obviously most imperfect, since what is intended here is an attempt to capture the life of an ever more complex on-going process evolving in time. Each step in our roadmap not only adds static structural features (as in the elementary school use of overheads) but connotes configurations of *affairs*, of additional on-going nexuses of activities of different sorts. The cumulative addition of these nexuses of activities in that particular sequence aims both at enriching the perspective, but also at triggering, with every new transparency being added, more and more encompassing questioning of the assumptions made in earlier steps, and some consequential continuous tinkering or *bricolage* with the earlier sets of assumptions and activities presented in earlier transparencies.

The first trio of layers (a, b, c) roughly connotes a phase of *appreciation and description*. The different steps define (a) the prerequisite attitude, discourse and vocabulary required for a meaningful inquiry to proceed; (b) the basic dynamics of the inquiry process that need to be initiated; and (c) the sort of mental map of the issue domain being explored, so as to anchor firmly the design thinking in the existing material and symbolic world of the issue domain.

The second trio of layers (d, e, f) corresponds roughly to *experimentation per se*. They correspond to the different stages of exploration in grappling with the new world to be constructed: (d) defines the forms that are adjusted to the circumstances and meet some basic conditions of goodness of fit; (e) explores their possibilities and acceptability with crucial partners; and then (f) develops workable prototypes by trial and error, in conversations with the prototypes and the partners, and in experiments.

The third trio of layers (g, h, i) focuses more on *learning per se*. This is the moment (g) when the learning loops crystallize and when multiple reference metrics emerge; (h) when the engagement of the different partners evolves, moral contracts among partners take hold, and a new discourse takes form that allows the conversation to establish itself on a new basis; and, (i) when a new appreciation of the internal and external constraints (on the conversation being conducted and on the selection of the prototypes likely to be most effective) emerges and gains traction.

This somewhat artificial partitioning and stylization has two main advantages: (a) it underlines clearly that, as one proceeds from Stage 1 to Stage 2, Stage 2 forces considerable recasting of Stage 1 assumptions and activities, and as one proceeds to Stage 3, some trigger is bound to force some recasting of the two earlier phases; and, (b) it provides the basis for a modest checklist that might serve as a useful guidepost in the evolution of the design process.

Design attitude: why, what and how

The different steps and stages in this design process are anything but linear, since feedback loops are constantly in action. But the new design attitude permeates all these stages and steps. First we explain why the change in attitude is so important. Then we define exactly what is accomplished in preparing the ground for effective design thinking. Third, we indicate how to proceed to engineer what is expected.

Why

One is not always as fully aware as one should be of the mental prisons haunting the sort of organizational culture in good currency, or the conventional wisdom that is crippling the work of all stakeholders as potential organization designers. One of the most important mental prisons is the focus on decision.

The focus on decision, as Boland and Collopy suggest, has led to people being completely mesmerized by a concern about choice among existing alternatives, on the assumption that the problem is already well-defined, and the possible alternatives well known. This is usually not the case. The design attitude recognizes that the problem definition has to be constructed, and that alternatives have to be created and crafted, and that they cannot be assumed to exist *ab ovo*. A course of action aims at creating better alternatives than what would appear to be originally available.[27]

In order to deal with an approach based on exploring systems which do not exist, what is required is not only a *different attitude* that single out these dimensions for careful attention but also a *different vocabulary* to tackle them. Boland and Collopy have already tried their hand at a provisional version of the new sort of lexicon:[28] collaboration, dialogue, improvisation, prototype, etc. These notions are essential in the designer's mental tool box.

In all organizations (private, public and social), the central basic challenge is *problem definition*. Each stakeholder has his own partial definition of the problem at hand, based on his partial knowledge and particular interests, but these partial and truncated views hardly suffice to define the problems at hand satisfactorily. This mental prison generates a dangerous blindness that obviously leads to the sorts of action that are likely to be misguided when they are based on these partial, reified, myopic and uncertainty-denial views. Yet such views

---

[27] Richard J. Boland and Fred Collopy (eds.). 2004. *Managing by Design*. Stanford, CA: Stanford University Press, chapter 1; Tim Brown. 2009. *Change by Design*. New York, NY: Harper Business.

[28] Boland and Collopy, 2004, *op.cit.*, chapter 37.

often succeed in hijacking the problem definition process, and derailing any meaningful inquiry.

Recognizing the full extent of every stakeholder's ignorance, the limitations it entails for their capacity to define the problem adequately, and the danger of premature reification means that ready-made problem definition needs to be replaced by a process of inquiry into problem definition that recognizes that most of the time the problems are wicked: (1) the goals are not known, or are very ambiguous or not agreed to by the stakeholders, and (2) the means-ends relationships are highly uncertain and poorly understood.[29] The new awareness is a prerequisite for any meaningful inquiry.

What

The development of such a new attitude would call for something as dramatic, for those educating the organizational designers, as the reframing of management education in North America triggered by the Ford Foundation and the Carnegie Commission in the middle of the last century. This Ford/Carnegie reframing considerably strengthened the quantitative and analytic approaches, focusing a great deal on decision making. But there has been of late a serious questioning of the excesses that this Ford/Carnegie twist has led to, not only in management studies, but in the social sciences in general.[30]

Boland and Collopy have defined the basic elements of the design attitude that would seem to be required in our complex world. For them, "a design attitude views each project as an opportunity for invention that includes a questioning of basic assumptions and a resolve to leave the world a better place than we found it."[31] Indeed, their 2004 book was planned to encourage a shift from a *decision* attitude to a *design* attitude.

The design attitude focuses on stewarding the inquiring system toward inventing assemblages of arrangements likely to foster better wayfinding and resilience. To accomplish that feat,

---

[29] Rittel and Webber, 1973, *op.cit.*

[30] William H. Starbuck. 2006. *The Production of Knowledge*. Oxford, UK: Oxford University Press.

[31] Boland and Collopy, 2004, *op.cit.*, p. 9.

it is necessary to focus on the meso-level. Organizations and institutions are meso-phenomena, too often poorly described and apprehended, because observers insist on looking at them through micro-perspectives that focus exclusively on individuals as absolutes, and deny the importance of relationships between entities. They are equally poorly understood by approaches focusing exclusively on macro-systems and totalities as absolutes. Organization design requires a vocabulary and an approach that focus at the meso-level.

Some exploratory work has already begun to develop not only some modest general propositions about the nature of the combinations of attributes likely to generate the most value-adding arrangements, given the circumstances, but also about what might be a workable approach to gauging whether these propositions hold under different circumstances: for example, when should the focus be on efficiency or innovation as the prevalent guiding force, as might be the case in the current protocols that would appear to dominate the process of design of organizational forms.[32]

How

As I have indicated elsewhere,[33] the new competencies and skills that need to be developed have much to do with *savoir-faire*, *savoir-être* and learning by doing. Such competencies, based on practical knowledge, have tended to be greatly underrated in a world where technical rationality has wrongly become hegemonic: presuming that knowledge flows only one way – from underlying disciplines to applied science to actual performance of services to clients and society. Substituting for this one-way street, a two-way approach, emphasizing knowing-in-action, reflection-in-action[34] (where knowledge emerges equally well from

---

[32] Anna Granderi and Santi Furnari. 2008. "A Chemistry of Organization: Combinatory Analysis and Design," *Organization Studies*, 29(3): 459-485.

[33] Gilles Paquet. 2009. *Crippling Epistemologies and Governance Failures— A Plea for Experimentalism*. Ottawa, ON: The University of Ottawa Press, chapter 2.

[34] Donald N. Michael et al. 1980. *The New Competence – The Organization as a Learning System*. San Francisco, CA: Values and Lifestyles Program.

groping with situations and from surprises leading to on-the-spot experiments and knowledge creation) is, at least ideally, the way professionals are educated.[35]

It emphasizes the development of skills and a capacity for a conversation with the situation through reflective practicum (residency, articling, etc.). It is seen to be the only way to impart practical knowledge in a manner that aims at nothing less than transformation and behaviour modification, for some of those skills are literally *embodied*: *savoir-faire* in the sense of *tour de main* cannot be learned and developed without a change in *savoir-être*, in identity.

It has proved extremely difficult to ensure the requisite training and coaching in these new competencies, for they require the development of perception skills, diagnostic skills and the like. This explains the explosion of parallel training ventures dealing with those areas dramatically neglected by the formal education enterprise.

Organization design uses a variety of mechanisms to help institute a living organization that has the capacity to be reliable but innovative, and to be resilient but able to learn. It aims at coherence, but mainly at dynamism. This cannot be accomplished by only tinkering with the hard dimensions of organizations (architecture and routines); it must also modify their behaviour and culture. Moreover, depending on circumstances, this sort of intervention will have to be sequenced carefully if it is to be successful.

This is an especially daunting task in the case of the exploration/exploitation split that often underpins the innovation/reliability challenge.[36] It is impossible to tackle this challenge without explicit efforts to transform the culture of the organization. The simple partitioning of tasks or efforts is unlikely to work.

---

[35] Herbert A. Simon. 1969/1981. *The Sciences of the Artificial.* Cambridge, MA: The MIT Press, chapter 5.

[36] James G. March. 1991. "Exploration and Exploitation in Organizational Learning," *Organization Science*, (2): 71-87.

Some principles have proved useful in this sort of work:[37]
- maximum participation to ensure the tapping of all relevant knowledge and more collaboration;
- subsidiarity, or the delegation of decision making to the most local level possible;
- some competition to squeeze out organizational slack and promote innovation; and
- multistability, i.e., the partitioning of the organization into sub-systems so as to be able to delegate to the one most able to handle a shock or perturbation the task of doing so, without the other sub-systems being forced to transform.

As for the most useful mechanisms, they have been:
- the setting up of ever more inclusive forums for effective multilogue;
- the negotiation of moral contracts defining clearly and well, yet informally, the mutual expectations of the different partners;
- the design of learning loops enabling the partners to revise their choices of means as the experience unfolds, but also to revise the very ends pursued through reframing the organization when it proves necessary; and,
- the invention of fail-safe mechanisms to ensure that the multilogue does not degenerate into meaningless consensuses, and to prevent *saboteurs* from derailing the collective effort.

The designer must be ready to prototype and to tinker as the process unfolds, but no organization will permit that unless some action plan is first at least hinted at – providing some sense of the nature of the experiment.

Nadler and Tushman have suggested a blueprint and sequence for design that might serve as such a security

[37] Gilles Paquet. 2005. *The New Geo-Governance: A Baroque Approach*. Ottawa, ON: The University of Ottawa Press, chapter 8.

blanket.[38] Their work might be stylized as follows (taking liberties with their own sequencing, and taking into account our earlier analyses):

- organizational assessment: functioning, performance gaps
- design criteria: what the new design should accomplish
- groupings: options for general grouping
- coordination requirements: information-processing needs
- linking: linking mechanisms (formal and informal)
- properties and capabilities of the ensuing assemblages
- provisional analysis of impacts
- simulation of the way in which the design would play out in different circumstances: prototyping and serious play
- operational design, including detailed planning of implementation: support of key power groups, rewarding desired behaviour, monitoring transition
- organizational culture (values, beliefs and norms) as means and ends
- social learning loop mechanisms as a way to adapt

Shifting attitude

It is not easy to capture a shift in attitude, yet it has been possible to detect such a shift in recent times on the part of those who have recognized that, in the new world of complexity and turbulence, forecasting has degenerated into future babble.[39] The attitude has had to change – from a focus on futile forecasting to a focus on developing effective coping protocols that would avoid the brunt of the malefits associated with the sort of disasters ascribable to the unexpected: avalanches, black swans and the unconceivable.[40]

One interesting way in which the new attitude might be generated has been presented in Weick and Sutcliffe's

[38] David A. Nadler and Michael L. Tushman. 1997. *Competing by Design – The Power of Organizational Architecture*. New York, NY: Oxford University Press.

[39] Dan Gardner. 2010. *Future Babble*. Toronto, ON: McClelland & Stewart.

[40] Nassim N. Taleb. 2007. *The Black Swan – The Impact of the Highly Improbable*. New York, NY: Random House.

Managing the Unexpected.[41] They have identified principles guiding high-reliability organizations in the face of turbulent environments. Three of these principles help to improve sensitivity and capacity to react quickly to the unexpected, and two of them have to do with the capacity to contain the toxic impacts of these avalanches:

- preoccupation with failure;
- reluctance to simplify;
- sensitivity to operations;
- commitment to resilience; and,
- deference to expertise.

These principles are built on *mindfulness.*

Weick and Sutcliffe suggest that these capabilities may be audited, but they may also be nudged into becoming instituted into the organizational culture and may be managed through leveraging "small wins" into progress of the organizational culture toward greater mindfulness.

This is only one approach to developing the new attitude required to be able to react helpfully to the unexpected. It may not be optimal in all cases either: some may even be repelled, for instance, by the authors' seemingly immense deference to the expertise dimension — a sentiment I would share.

Other stratagems have been put forward: either in the nature of an expedient shortcut like *catastrophisme éclairé à la* Dupuy – a ruse to deceive society into taking seriously the omens of disasters that would normally be ignored – a strong urge to mindfulness, unlikely to work in the long run; or in the nature of a plea for an entirely refurbished conceptual framework – *antifragility à la* Taleb calling for embracing uncertainty and disorder rather than trying in a futile way to eliminate them – a plea for a revolution in the mind also unlikely to materialize overnight.[42]

[41] Karl E. Weick and Kathleen M. Sutcliffe. 2007 (2nd ed.). *Managing the Unexpected – Resilient Performance in an Age of Uncertainty.* New York, NY: Wiley & Sons.

[42] Jean-Pierre Dupuy. 2002. *Pour un catastrophisme éclairé – Quand l'impossible est certain.* Paris, FR: Seuil; Nassim N. Taleb. 2012. *Antifragile – Things that Gain from Disorder.* New York, NY: Random House.

Neither of these alternative approaches would appear to be acceptable in the way that the Weick and Sutcliffe approach is. Yet the Weick and Sutcliffe approach also depends on cultural change to a certain extent and, therefore, requires much patience – even though "small wins" may indeed bring forth a change of attitude in much less than one generation. This will not be satisfactory for those calling for instant repairs, but it may well be the best one can expect.

One of the great merits of the Weick and Sutcliffe approach is that the authors have shown through a variety of cases that it can be very easily operationalized. Progress along the different axes defined by the basic principles can be gauged, and "small wins" along those axes can also be gauged in terms of simple questions. Consequently, even though the notion of mindfulness may be elusive to many, there is a sense that the avenue opened by Weick and Sutcliffe is promising. This is all the more so because the process that the authors have sketched need not be rigidly adopted. Other axes of mindfulness may be invented using the same protocol they suggest to gauge progress.

One of the most interesting possibilities opened by the Weick and Sutcliffe approach is that a whole range of economic, social and political entrepreneurs (who spot disharmonies between what seem to be the *rules* in good currency, and the sort of *practices* likely to be effective) may act on these anomalies that are the source of puzzlement. This is a job that does not rest entirely on leaders or other pseudo-masters of the game, who claim to be in charge, but on all those taking part in the game – anyone who may note these anomalies and may be able to intervene ever so slightly.

Conclusion

The process of organization design is not linear, but it is rather an iterative inquiry, a trial and error experiment, a search process. It is the sort of reflection-in-action that Donald Schön has so aptly described – a conversation with the situation that leads to discovery.[43]

[43] Donald A. Schön, 1983, *op. cit.*

At the core of this process is the inquiring mind, the designer paying attention to the evolving environment, a multiple-looped learning through which ends, means and assumptions are continually revised as the experiment proceeds – in the way that the Inuit artist scrapes away at a reindeer antler with his knife, examining it first from one angle and then from another, until he cries out, "Ah, seal!"[44]

In this sort of inquiry, it has often proved easier to tinker with the technology than with the structure, and easier to tinker with the structure than with the culture of the organization.[45] But it would be unwise to presume that any particular sequence will always work.

The reaction to puzzles is too often to ignore them, and to pursue the on-going tasks as usual, instead of being startled by the anomalies: recognizing that they are creating mysteries; being compelled to find *ways of understanding mysteries;* and searching for guidelines to solve a mystery by the organized exploration of possibilities.[46]

Alert individuals become more aware of marginal practices (or alternative ways to re-tool, re-structure and reframe their activities, according to principles heretofore not necessarily regarded as of central interest) and they tend to become involved in lateral thinking: articulating the problem differently, cross-appropriating ways of doing things elsewhere, adjusting them to the task at hand, and reframing the very notion of the business one is in.

It is the world of prototyping, of experimentation, of serious play, of organization design. Innovative persons in all areas (economic, political, social, etc.) become organization designers and redefine the style of their organization.

Whether the design attitude will come to replace the decision focus easily and soon is an open question, but it is the fundamental next step. What makes it particularly difficult is that the design attitude entails not only a different perspective,

[44] Donald A. Schön and Martin Rein. 1994. *Frame Reflection.* New York, NY: Basic Books, p. 166-167.

[45] Donald A. Schön. 1971. *Beyond the Stable State.* New York, NY: Norton.

[46] Roger Martin. 2004. "The Design of Business," *Rotman Magazine,* winter, p. 7.

but a shift *from a reactive posture vis-à-vis* a more or less placid environment to a *proactive engagement* to transform the situation. This is an action that requires capabilities that are not necessarily part of the arsenal of dispassionate positivist analysts.

The only way to develop this new design attitude is to try it out, to develop prototypes, to play with them and, in so doing, to elicit ways in which effective stewardship may be designed.[47] That is the task of Part II of this book.

---

[47] For particular examples of successful efforts in practicing stewardship as "the art of aligning decisions with impact when many minds are involved in making a plan, and many hands in enacting it," see Bryan Boyer, Justin W. Cook and Marco Steinberg. 2013. *Legible Practises – Six Stories about the Craft of Stewardship*. Helsinki, Finland: Helsinki Design Lab/SITRA.

PART II

Wicked Trans-scientific
Policy Challenges

We are, as Brian Arthur would put it, in a world "where beliefs, strategies and actions of agents are being 'tested' for survival within a situation or outcome or 'ecology' that these beliefs, strategies and actions together create. […] agents are not just reacting to a problem, they are trying to make sense of it; their very actions in doing so collectively re-form the current outcome, which requires them to adjust afresh."[1] Our approach in this book explores 'a world in formation,' as it searches for a way to elicit wayfinding in a world where the overall process is a self-creating one.

The three complex wicked policy problems examined in Part II have developed around contested concepts. They have evolved in somewhat different ways and generated different sets of arrangements through different crystallizations of perspectives, beliefs and ideologies.

The notion of equality, discussed in chapter 4, has become such a fixture of the democratic ethos, and has been by now so well rooted in our mores, that a strong version of it – egalitarianism – has become the dominant ideology. The epidemic of entitlements underpinning 'democracy' may have generated immensely toxic effects on the common public culture, but it remains a basic reference. Consequently, the alternative that is put forward here – equability – is still facing an extraordinary uphill battle.

The notion of diversity, discussed in chapter 5, has elicited a policy response in Canada – multiculturalism – that has become the basis of a crusade presenting it as the optimal policy for pluralist societies. This national policy has had some level of toxic impact on the common public culture in our fragile society. The state propaganda about maximum diversity being optimal diversity, and about multiculturalism being the panacea has succeeded in hoodwinking a plurality of Canadians, at least temporarily.

The notion of sustainability, discussed in chapter 6, has still not congealed into a tractable concept. It has spawned a

[1] W. Brian Arthur. 2013. *Complexity Eonomics: A Different Framework for Economic Thought*. Santa Fe Institute, Working Paper, April 12, p. 5.

variety of perspectives that have not yet blended harmoniously. It has been agreed that there is no technical answer, and that collaboration and social learning are likely to evolve some tractable ways to accommodate the diverse points of view, but the matter remains fundamentally unsettled. Even the general direction in which a viable organizational learning regime might evolve is not clear. Groping mechanisms are still the flavour of the day.

Three wicked policy problems: different settings, different wayfinding processes, different ideological grips, different stages in the blending of perspectives, but a resembling set of wicked trans-scientific policy issues.

| Equality

"... democratic peoples ... have an ardent, insatiable, eternal,
invincible passion for equality; they want equality in liberty,
and, if they cannot obtain it, they still want it in slavery."

Alexis de Tocqueville

Introduction

*T*he *Wealth of Nations* – the foundational work of Adam Smith on the invisible hand that promotes the view that coordination may be ensured by an invisible hand in market economies – was always meant by Smith to be read in parallel with his *Theory of Moral Sentiments,* his foundational work on morality. It is the second and equally important invisible hand that is meant to ensure that the moral underground of socio-economies will keep society within a corridor that prevents excesses capable of throwing the market economies out of whack. Both coordination mechanisms were seen by Adam Smith as necessary to ensure socio-economic peace and progress.

Over the last 70 years, immense attention has been given to the first invisible hand, the one celebrated in the first book, and this has often led to the message of the second invisible hand being occluded and ignored. This willful blindness to ethico-cultural considerations has been encouraged by the positivist ideology in good currency in the social sciences in the 20th century – an ideology in which any reference to normative dimensions was regarded as out of bounds. This Manichean attitude has considerably undermined the work of social scientists, especially as redistributive state interventions have grown exponentially in the name of egalitarianism, and have had both positive and negative effects on both the workings of the market economies and on their cultural and moral undergrounds.

While the beneficial stabilizing effects of redistributive initiatives over the cycle have been celebrated in the short run, their negative longer term impacts on both the workings of the market economies, and on the decay of their cultural and moral undergrounds, have been ignored. Indeed, those who have drawn attention to such long-term malefits have often been brutally rebuffed as anti-progressive – a deadly label in some intellectual quarters, where *progressive* has come to connote any stance based on self-righteousness and public compassion, that is thereby exonerated from having to demonstrate its effectiveness and forgiven for its toxicity.

In 2012, we were reminded sharply of the taboos attached to any critical statement about the quest for equality through redistribution. The most notable quotation of that year (according to Fred Shapiro, the associate librarian at the Yale Law School on December 11, 2012) was the statement by Mitt Romney (the Republican presidential candidate in the 2012 American federal election) that 47 percent of the US population have now become somewhat permanently dependent on government transfers, and are 'on the take', so to speak. This quotation, secretly recorded at a fundraiser meeting in May 2012, was posted in September 2012 by *Mother Jones* magazine, and is regarded by many as a statement that may have cost Romney the presidency of the United States.

Whether the percentage is correct or not, and whether this quotation was the cause of Romney's loss or not is not the point here. Rather, it is about how inconvenient it is to ever raise questions about the way in which redistribution may possibly have negative external effects, and may have generated a culture of entitlement in our society, thereby eroding the citizen's sense of self-reliance, independence and responsibility. Entitlements have become a sort of second nature for the citizens of Western democracies, akin to sacred cows. Former Canadian Liberal federal minister David Dingwall made use of this conviction in the hearts of citizens in his famous statement, when questioned about some unusual reimbursements of expenditures he demanded when he was Master of the Mint – "I am entitled to my entitlements" – a statement that was meant to close the discussion. And most citizens would appear to share this view about entitlements – however they have come about, and however rationally indefensible they might be when the full details of the circumstances are explained. Indeed, anyone bold enough to challenge entitlements does so at his peril.

This chapter is about the dark side of the notion of *equality* when elevated to the stance of *egalitarianism* – or the dogmatic search for equality of outcomes – and, consequently, of the notion of income and wealth redistribution, both when it interferes toxically with the workings of our socio-economies, and when it generates a culture of entitlements that erodes the character of our citizens. And it is about the way in which we may usefully reflect on the governance of *equability* – a notion we suggest is less toxic than egalitarianism.

First, it throws some light on the sociology of equality as expounded by Alexis de Tocqueville in the 19th century. Second, briefly, it sketches the process that has led to the exponential growth of governmental *gratifications* and to their hardening into a cumulative ratcheting of non-negotiable entitlements or *acquis*. Third, it examines the ways in which such a drift may have had positive effects in the shorter and medium terms on socio-economies experiencing sharp business cycles, but has also had a toxic effect in the longer term on the burden of office of citizens as governors – increasing irresponsibility, disengagement and victimology. Fourth, since *egalitarianism* is the philosophy underpinning this entitlement edifice and entitlement drive, an argument is made in favour of replacing it with a philosophy of *equability* as an alternative foundational anchor. Finally, the chapter outlines what the governance of equability might look like.

The Tocqueville mechanism[1]

Alexis de Tocqueville has shown that *"les peuples démocratiques … ont pour l'égalité une passion ardente, insatiable, éternelle, invincible; ils veulent l'égalité dans la liberté et, s'ils ne peuvent l'obtenir, ils la veulent encore dans l'esclavage."*[2]

The core of *De la démocratie en Amérique II* (the 1840 book) is a sort of sociology of equality in democratic societies. It argues that the basis of modernity and democracy is rooted in this sentiment of equality.

Equality in the sense of Tocqueville is not an observed fact, but it is fundamentally an ideal, an "imaginary equality", an egalitarianism that drives democracy.[3] Tocqueville has shown that equality is not only the dominant value in democracy, but that *"le désir de l'égalité devient toujours plus insatiable à mesure que l'égalité est plus grande:"*[4] even when a very egalitarian status has been realized in a society, *"on peut compter que chacun de ses citoyens apercevra toujours près de soi plusieurs points qui le dominent, et l'on peut prévoir qu'il tournera obstinément ses regards de ce seul côté."*[5] So, contrary to what one might have suspected, greater equality does not generate less envy, but more.

This sort of passion for equality applies as well to ethnic and cultural groups. And it works with even more force when there is a coexistence of decreed egalitarian rights with considerable *de facto* differences in power, wealth, etc. among the different groups. Strong *resentment* ensues. It leads not only

---

[1] This section draws freely from Paul Laurent and Gilles Paquet. 1991. "Intercultural Relations: A Myrdal-Tocqueville-Girard Interpretative Scheme," *International Political Science Review,* 12(3): 171-183.

[2] Alexis de Tocqueville. 1961 (1840). *De la démocratie en Amérique.* Paris, FR: Gallimard, (Edition Mayer), vol. II, p. 104.

[3] *Ibid.*, p. 189.

[4] *Ibid.*, p. 144.

[5] Tocqueville quoted in Paul Dumouchel and Jean-Pierre Dupuy. 1979. *L'enfer des choses.* Paris, FR: Seuil, p. 49.

to cultural jealousies (an innocuous zeal in the preservation of something possessed), but to envy (defined as displeasure and ill-will at the superiority of another person in happiness, success, reputation or the possession of anything desirable).

The rise of egalitarianism as a modern democratic dogma, and the concomitant acceleration of the global demographic shuffling process, have consequently produced a heightened degree of tension, frustration and envy at the intercultural interface. It has contributed to the accumulation of culture-specific social capital, and to the further balkanization of modern societies. Moreover, in countries like Canada, where multiculturalism has become a national policy, and where cultural rights have become entrenched in charters and laws, the process of segmentation has been accentuated, and envy has been further promoted in view of the stark contrast between the equality of ethno-cultural groups decreed as the norm, and the realities of intercultural differences.[6]

The transformation of the socio-economic process over the last century has also fostered this passion for equality. In a poor society, consumption is concentrated on basic material goods. However, when the standard of living rises, the demand for luxury goods and positional goods increases. Competition for positional goods is underpinned by a passion for distinction, for resources in absolute scarcity that bestow upon individuals possessing them some relative superiority. "The distinctive appurtenances of the rich then become squirrel's wheels for those below: objects of desire that the most intensive effort cannot reach."[7] The increase in the relative importance of positional competition has heightened the relative frustration of those on the lower rungs, increased resentment and made the whole socio-economic process more envy-driven.

[6] Gilles Paquet. 1989. "Multiculturalism as National Policy," *Journal of Cultural Economics*, 13: 17-34.

[7] Fred Hirsch. 1976. *Social Limits to Growth*. Cambridge, MA: Harvard University Press, p. 66.

The dynamics of the entitlement revolution

In a world of surprises, accelerated change, and necessary adaptation and adjustments to constantly changing circumstances, the quest for stability and certainty may be illusory, but it is a constant human aspiration. It has inspired a variety of strategies by individuals and groups to immunize themselves from the vagaries of the environment by all sorts of contraptions. Some of these contraptions have been insurance schemes of various sorts to alleviate the dramatic impacts of unforeseen tragedies, or to prevent the miseries attached to gross inconveniences, like the abrupt interruption of earnings. Such schemes (private, public or social) have not eliminated uncertainty, but they have mitigated the destructive effects of unpredictable tragedies.

Over time, the natural preference for not having one's life disturbed has come to be regarded as a widely-shared reasonable preference-cum-expectation. This legitimate quest for certainty has induced many individuals and groups (with the complicity of governments, which are always seeking ways to please more and more active and vocal citizens, and obtain their electoral support) to allow these preferences for certainty to be transubstantiated into some version of human rights, and those rights to be translated into the entitlements of citizens to have protection from undesirable circumstances provided by their governments.

When compounded with the egalitarian ethos that breeds envy, the welfare state doctrine, where not only needs but preferences are to be met, has been toxic. The egalitarian doctrine has preached that any citizen *qua* citizen is as meritorious and deserving as the next one, and this has made it possible to regard as odious any form of differential outcome. Indeed, it has been argued that if one cannot have access to a service, neither should anyone else – all in the name of equality of outcome. This means that entitlements have come to be not only related to basic needs, but also and most vociferously to positional goods: one should not have to suffer that others are allowed to avail themselves of goods or services that one is not able to access. Envy has become a barometer of legitimate expectations, and any form of inequality denounced as fundamentally illegitimate.

Once preferences have been articulated as rights and entitlements, they quickly crystallize into a set of guarantees that come to be regarded as having been earned (*des acquis*) and they are thus expected to be provided by the state in perpetuity. Moreover, any existing platform of *acquis* in good currency at any one time quickly becomes the legitimate basis from which it can be expected that additional protections might be added in due time – down the wish list of the United Nations 1947 Universal Declaration of Human Rights, and more.

This sort of progressive ratcheting up has acquired such sanctimonious respect that any attempt to renegotiate a previous arrangement in light of changing circumstances, or of the discovery of unintended toxic consequences (financial or behavioural) as a result of previous engagements, has come to be regarded as *de facto* unacceptable for any reason.

The cumulative effect of some 50 years of such entitlements – something that Nicholas Eberstadt has referred to as an *"entitlement epidemic"*[8] – has been an exponential increase of state transfers to individuals. A growing dependency of citizens on such transfers, and the parallel growth of a culture of entitlements would appear to make this increase likely to continue unabated. The result will be possible toxic effects on governments for whom this may become unaffordable, and on the citizens themselves for whom such arrangements may generate malefits in the form of learned dependency and helplessness, of an erosion of their burden of office as citizens, and even of their *moral character* as members of a liberal democracy.

Indeed, moral agency has been undermined as governments have started to take over tasks that individuals used to do themselves. The very idea of *vulnerability* "has become such a cannibal that it now covers not only

[8] Nicholas Eberstadt. 2012. *A Nation of Takers – America's Entitlement Epidemic*. West Conshohocken, PA: Templeton Press.

the victims of misfortune or delinquency but even the delinquents themselves."[9]

Impacts of the entitlement revolution

The progressive intelligentsia denies any negative impact of the entitlement epidemic. Yet there is much evidence of negative impacts on all fronts (affordability, perverse incentives, market distortions and moral vacancy). Well intentioned and generosity-inspired transfer mechanisms (like inter-regional equalization payments or region-based unemployment insurance benefits to reward more generously, and in a semi-permanent way, the unemployed in hard-pressed regions) have been shown to deter inter-regional migration, and to lead to higher rates of unemployment and social welfare recipients than what would otherwise have materialized.[10] At the very time when such transfers have come to be regarded as indispensable, they have also become unaffordable, and regarded by experts as deterring growth, being self-defeating, and generating pure waste.[11]

Discussions about these issues have led to an increased recognition that mechanisms of equalization, fuelled by the egalitarian spirit, have a dual effect: to allay the inconveniences of unfortunate circumstances in the short run; and, especially if the benefits are unduly generous, to slow down the process of adaptation to such circumstances (e.g., adjustment in location or in the skills matrix), and possibly to generate additional and more serious and deeper malefits in the long run, if the capacity to adapt is significantly thwarted.

This new awareness has called for a balancing of these positive and negative effects in the assessment of the ever larger number of equalizing and redistribution schemes that have been put in place over the last 50 years. Economists have generally stood in stark opposition to the egalitarianism drive

[9] Kenneth Minogue. 2010. *The Servile Mind*. London, UK: Encounter Books, p. 9.

[10] Thomas J. Courchene. 1981. "A Market Perspective on Regional Disparities," *Canadian Public Policy*, VII(4): 506-518.

[11] Jean-Luc Migué and Gérard Bélanger. 2013. "Interregional Growth Divergence and Living Standards Convergence," *The Independent Review*, 17(3): 369-377.

propounded by the progressives: for them, such schemes are likely to have toxic impacts on the behaviour of individuals or groups being thereby dissuaded from adjusting as much or as quickly as they might otherwise have. Incentives matter.

The progressives' view has come to be regarded not only as the view in good currency, but also as the only defensible view in the common public culture. Sixty years of ideological programming have made it politically incorrect to acknowledge (or even to mention) that some behavioural modification might be ascribable to perverse incentive reward systems, rooted in excessively generous and indiscriminate redistribution schemes that were put in place in the name of egalitarianism.

A Keynesian case for temporary transfers in time and space

The notion of redistributive mechanisms, either inter-regionally or over the business cycle, to ensure system stability, has been in good currency for the past 60 years. Indeed, it has been suggested that some of the European economic problems these days are ascribable to the fact that Europe did not manage to put in place arrangements to recycle surpluses among countries, and thereby ensure system stability.[12]

While such mechanisms are not guaranteed to work well and most effectively all the time, and while there may be reasons for them to operate better or worse under certain conditions, they usually have done some good at ensuring system stability in the shorter run. Even in the case of Canada, which has experienced disparity among resource-rich provinces and others, fine-tuning such redistribution schemes has proven useful in unusually difficult circumstances. So the short-term benefits of such automatic stabilizers or equalization schemes are not generally fundamentally questioned. Some critics have questioned the effectiveness of inter-regional redistribution schemes in the medium term and it has been recognized that they may not work as well as expected all the time.

---

[12] Yanis Varoufakis. 2011. *The Global Minotaur*. London, UK: Zed Books.

Our concern here is the impact of redistribution schemes in time and space, leading to long-term dependency on government transfers by a large portion of the population, and thereby leading to behavioural changes by individuals and groups.

The standard argument, pointing to the market distortions and inefficiencies generated by such schemes, is well known, and has been forcefully made by Thomas Courchene. The Courchene argument was hotly contested in the 1980s.[13] Courchene's contentions were not denied, but they were side-swiped by 'progressive' arguments that conjectured that the *inefficiency losses* were more than compensated for by the *growth effect* of the redistributive schemes. No proof was ever marshaled for this contention: the moral superiority of the redistribution argument was considered sufficient.

Not all distortions are innocuous

More recently, Nicholas Eberstadt has added some flats and sharps to the Keynesian argument: the entitlement epidemic may transform some liberal democracies into "nations of takers," and this is in the process of eroding the character of self-reliant citizens in a country like the United States.

The Eberstadt argument moved the debate squarely to the moral ground. It suggested that the entitlement epidemic was not only undermining the work of the invisible hand of the market, but that it had been destructive of the moral fibre of the citizenry.[14] This argument was attacked by progressives who suggested, somewhat unpersuasively, that 'taking' was not a problem, and certainly did not lead to dependence.[15]

It is clear that not all aspects of the entitlement epidemic can be ascribed to the implementation of entirely indefensible arrangements. Many redistribution schemes have responded

[13] Donald J. Savoie. 1986. "Courchene and Regional Development: Beyond the Neo-classical Approach," *Canadian Journal of Regional Science*, IX(1): 69-77.

[14] Nicholas Eberstadt. 2012. "American Character at Stake," *The Wall Street Journal*, September 1, C1.

[15] William A. Galston. 2012. "Have we become a nation of takers?" in N. Eberstadt, *op.cit.*, p. 93-113.

to new problems (ageing), and to new expectations that are not unreasonable in a richer society (health, education, etc., especially when one is dealing with public goods – i.e., those where the social benefits are greater than the private benefits, and where there is a danger of underinvestment since the person investing can only capture a portion of the benefits engendered). Moreover, not all aspects of the welfare state have necessarily contributed to the growing moral vacancy. Other factors may, in part, explain the growth of entitlements and the new dependency on government transfers. But it is quite ostrich-like to deny that much of the underlying wave of entitlements has taken root very deeply in a new culture of rights, and that it is unlikely to be self-correcting.

In fact, the silent but fundamental tinkering by the state with the process of distribution of income and wealth over the past 60 years has had a first set of distorting effects on the production and finance processes (that Courchene has underlined), and economic inefficiency has ensued. But it has also had a second set of distorting effects on the ecology of social groups and their motivations (that Eberstadt has underlined), and an erosion of the moral basis of the social compact is emerging from this second set of distortions.[16]

The first set of distortions has been reluctantly conceded and rationalized as the social inefficiency cost that we should be willing to pay to ensure a more human and collaborative *vivre-ensemble* – the efficiency cost of living in a decent and civilized society.[17]

The second one has generated much more unease, and has met with a much starker denial, because it points to the erosion of the social compact itself (even though William Galston

---

[16] For an analysis of the socio-economy as an instituted process in terms of sub-processes like production, finance, state, demography, distribution of income and wealth, and the ecology of social groups and their motivations, see Gilles Paquet. 2009. "MRI for an arterio-sclerotic socio-economy," in G. Paquet. *Scheming virtuously – The road to collaborative governance*. Ottawa, ON: Invenire, p. 45-54.

[17] Avishai Margalit. 1996. *The Decent Society*. Cambridge, MA: Harvard University Press.

strenuously denies it), and of the reciprocity and solidarity on which our society is built, and its replacement by a form of dependency that is much more akin to voluntary servitude than to solidarity.

Indeed, the second set of distortions cannot really be as easily rationalized as the first one. Compensation schemes may be envisaged and designed to correct the toxic disincentives that ensue from redistributive schemes on the production and finance systems, but such schemes cannot easily be envisaged when the second type of distortions in the socio-ethical underground generates changes in belief systems and behaviour, and causes a form of disengagement and greater irresponsibility.

In the latter case, there is a sense of irreversibility when there is a discontinuous shift – from a state of affairs where we deal with temporary inconveniences that we might wish to attenuate, to a state of affairs where inconveniences have to be eliminated as a matter of right. This sort of rights or entitlements inflation both debases the legitimacy of the defensible core of human rights, and also makes this inflation immensely more difficult to debunk once it has acquired entitlement status. The language of rights and entitlements does not lend itself easily to discussion and compromise: once something is claimed as a right or an entitlement, the conversation is all but terminated.[18]

This irreversibility makes the entitlement epidemic one of great consequence. In the absence of a crisis or its equivalent, it is most unlikely that a new philosophy can develop the capability to contain the epidemic and to reduce the harm it generates. Yet, without such a new philosophy, it is unlikely that the necessary reframing of perspectives, and the necessary transformation of the ruling cosmology and belief system, can be accomplished.

The entitlement epidemic has made a dent in the common public culture and in the moral order, and it has transformed the set of assumptions and beliefs on which our notion of *vivre-ensemble* is built. The correctives required cannot only

[18] Michael Ignatieff. 2001. *Human Rights as Politics and Idolatry*. Princeton, NJ: Princeton University Press.

build on some changes in the plumbing of the socio-economy: they must expose the assumptions and question the beliefs that are at the basis of the cosmology in good currency at this time.

The toxicity of the entitlement epidemic

The entitlement epidemic has been regarded by many as an innocuous modification of the technology of the state/income-and-wealth distribution subsystems. In fact, this change in the state/income-and-wealth distribution subsystems has impacted not only the production/finance subsystems (the Courchene effect), but also, and more profoundly, the ecology of social groups and their motivations (the Eberstadt effect). As a result of these impacts, the entire social system (technology, structure and theory)[19] has been modified. It would therefore be futile to try to initiate simple technological fixes or structural correctives to tame these toxic effects of the entitlement epidemic on the ethos. Nothing less than an all-out effort to transform the way the social system envisages its purposes and its future will do.

While it may be clear that the common public culture has been eroded by the entitlement epidemic, and that this epidemic has been bolstered to a great extent by state excesses, it is necessary also to be clear about the forces at work in civil society before an effective set of correctives can be designed.

The weakening of the common public culture
This is not the place to develop a full theory of civil society and its foundations. However, it is not possible to reflect on what might be a useful strategy to correct the toxic impacts of the entitlement epidemic without putting this problem in context.

The evolution of the texture of a socio-economy as an instituted process may be considered as a chronicle of the armistices between the geo-technical constraints defining the

---

[19] An organization or a social system contains structure, theory and technology: a set of roles and relations among members; the views held by members about its purposes, its operations, its environment and its future; and the prevailing technology of the system reflecting and influencing both structure and theory. Donald A. Schön. 1971. *Beyond the Stable State*. New York, NY: Random House.

material realities, and the values and plans of individuals and groups attempting to impose their preferences and wishes on it. This takes the form of human contraptions of all sorts, originally designed to create new forms of reconciliations among the families of pressures, but then these contraptions develop their own dynamics. This definition of the socio-economy as instituted process, *à la* Karl Polanyi,[20] may usefully be mapped onto a triangle identifying at each of its apexes one major principle of integration – economy (market exchange), polity (hierarchy or coercion), and society or civil society (solidarity or network) – with the possibility of mixed arrangements combining these principles. Such a triangle, inspired by the work of Kenneth Boulding,[21] can be visualized in Figure 4.

FIGURE 4

The Adapted Boulding Triangle

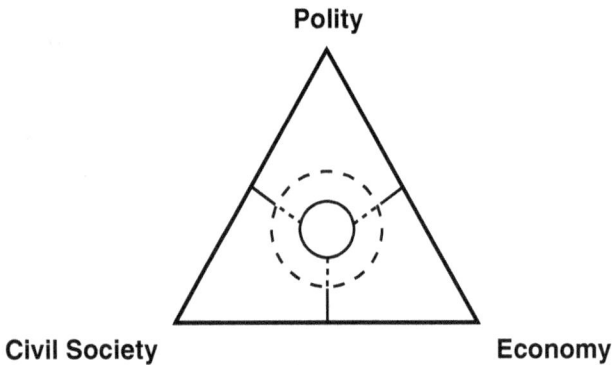

Polity

Civil Society

Economy

For any particular socio-economy, the centre of gravity may at any particular time be closer to one of the apexes, and through time, this centre of gravity may evolve in certain directions. For instance, the development of the welfare state and the growth of the state in the second half of the

[20] Karl Polanyi. 1957. "The Economy as Instituted Process" in K. Polanyi et al. *Trade and Markets in the Early Empires*. New York, NY: The Free Press, p. 243-270.

[21] Kenneth E. Boulding. 1970. *A Primer on Social Dynamics*. New York, NY: The Free Press.

20th century, have nudged the texture of socio-economies of Western Europe towards a greater role for the hierarchy/ coercion arrangements in the polity, and a lesser role for the other two organizational principles.

The entitlement epidemic (originating with the state's decisions to transubstantiate some preferences into rights that the state has to honour) has resulted in the role of the polity in the Boulding triangle being increased, and it has crowded out activities that were previously handled by the other two mechanisms. This has led to an erosion of the common public culture (i.e., of the civil society's capacity to handle these activities). This erosion of the common public culture has in some way undermined and weakened the social and moral foundations – the character – of the society in question.[22]

The debates around the Eberstadt thesis have centred on the source of the common public culture – or, to use a slightly different vocabulary, on the social capital enabling the society to perform all sorts of enabling functions. On the left, it has been argued that it is the redistribution functions of the state that are at the source of much of this social capital. On the right, it has been argued rather, that the market has been the source of social capital. As a matter of consequence, when confronted with the toxic impact of the entitlement epidemic on civil society, representatives of the left have at first denied any such toxic effect, and then have argued that increased state redistributive action should be used to refurbish social capital. Observers from the right have been more circumspect.

This caution is based on an old tradition going back to Montesquieu, Voltaire and de Tocqueville suggesting that market relations (*le doux commerce*) have been at the foundation of civil society, and that the role of civil society has been to limit the encroachment of the state on the operations of the socio-economy.

---

[22] For an illustration of this process of erosion of the common public culture in Quebec and the rest of Canada, see Gary Caldwell. 2012. *Canadian Public Culture*. Ste-Edwidge-de-Clifton, QC: Fermentation Press.

Weaker ties and equability

The idea of rebalancing the Boulding triangle by getting the state to pull back may be attractive to the right, but it is an abomination for the left, that regards solidarity as being produced by state redistribution, and the inter-regional and inter-group laundering of money. The great opacity of the production of social capital does not help in arbitrating these different contentions, but I think it is fair to say that intrusive state action is more likely to crowd-out solidarity.

One of the dirty little secrets nobody wishes to face is that the virtuous circle of more solidarity generating more redistribution generating more solidarity is broken. We have known for quite a while that inter-regional and inter-group laundering of money and other redistribution schemes have ceased to generate national solidarity (if indeed they ever did) except perhaps in the sermons of the progressives for whom it is an article of faith.

Redistribution may reduce the differences in levels of economic welfare, but the smaller the differences, the higher the tension. What has to be debunked is the sacred character of outcome-equalizing egalitarianism. Only its replacement by a weaker and softer notion is likely to lend itself to trade-offs. Equability may be a more useful reference.

This word — *equability* — is a term that Merriam-Webster defines as the "lack of noticeable, unpleasant, or extreme variation or inequality." The term focuses on finding the right balance in the practical search for a balance between equality, efficiency and fairness. Yet this is a word that is not in good currency in Canada, where terms like "entitlements" and "egalitarianism" — words that are quite legalistic and reek of non-negotiability — are the sort of reference points most often quoted.

A shift from egalitarianism to equability as a reference point would transform the doctrinaire position of the progressives from an either-or to a more-or-less framework. Instead of having to staunchly deny any possibility of trade-off between equality and other dimensions of interest like efficiency, etc., this would pose the challenge of how much egalitarianism needs to be abandoned to accommodate a requisite, but not absolute, degree of efficiency. Equability would raise the possibility of *acceptable inequalities*. This entails factoring in the psycho-social dimensions and the moral order, and finding ways to have some countervailing effect on the egalitarian system of beliefs and the cosmology that are now in vogue. In such a shift from an egalitarian to an equability cosmology, the code of honour may be the determining factor, making possible the transition from one system of beliefs to another, from one state of the common public culture (and the ultra-sociality or morality attached to it) to another.[23]

The governance of equability

The egalitarian illusions that have inspired, bolstered and supported the entitlement epidemic have been exposed for quite a long time.[24] It has been shown that "a society cannot long endure unless it rewards and protects its productive members, and punishes and curbs predators, cheaters, and free-riders."[25] But even if compassion is an indefensible basis for morality, it remains most seductive. Both Courchene and Eberstadt (among others) have shown that egalitarianism-inspired policies generate distortions in the workings of both invisible hands (market for Courchene and morality for Eberstadt) and have argued for taming the entitlement epidemic based on egalitarianism. It is fair to say that their message has not been heard.

---

[23] As Appiah would have it, social and moral revolutions often originate with a slippage in the code of honour. There obviously was a lag between the first nobleman responding to a dueling challenge by sending his valets to punish the insolent challenger, and the disappearance of dueling; or the first denunciation of slavery, and the abolition of slavery. But it may be that it is only when some egalitarian form of redistribution comes to be regarded – as it was once – as dishonourable, that it will be really possible to challenge egalitarian redistribution as an institution. K. Anthony Appiah. 2010. *The Honor Code*. New York, NY: Norton.

[24] John Kekes. 2003. *The Illusions of Egalitarianism*. Ithaca, NY: Cornell University Press.

[25] *Ibid.*, p. 206.

The difficulty is that these matters have been debated as a black and white dichotomy that appeared to leave no possibility for a compromise position between zero redistribution and indiscriminate and imprudently generous egalitarianism-inspired redistribution. What needs to be recognized is that modest and prudent redistribution, based on a philosophy of *equability* (i.e., a philosophy geared to eliminating unacceptable inequalities) may very well be a middle-of-the road position that could be defended as underpinning reasonable policy choices.

That would entail incurring efficiency (technical and social) costs, but only to the point where they would generate technical, social and moral benefits that would make such a choice defensible. This would hardly simplify the task, since there is a great amount of imprecision in the data that might help to ascertain what such a stance might mean in real-life situations. But it might be a sufficient guidepost to rein in the entitlement epidemic, and to help to tame it.

In the case of the first invisible hand (market), much discussion has already taken place that can guide the design of decisions as to how much redistribution is optimal – for instance, over the business cycle to make the intervention worth the trouble. It is much more difficult when it comes to redistributing across groups or between generations, but, except for unrepentant ideologues, there is at least some ground for meaningful conversations.

In the case of the second invisible hand (morality) – a territory already broached when one deals with redistribution across groups and generations – the debate is still stuck in Manichean positions, and even the legitimacy of the question of how far redistribution should proceed would not appear to be agreed upon. There is probably a certain degree of redistribution through entitlements that can be defended in terms of economic, social and moral net benefits. But equally much of what is going on is indefensible by this sort of standard. The fact that a serious debate is systematically avoided may be ascribable to the fact that no single position can be defended in completely persuasive ways in the abstract, but also because the different actors use different reference points and *ordres de grandeur* to defend their positions (e.g., utilitarian or egalitarian gauges, for instance).

But the notion that there might be trade-offs that might be regarded as acceptable to different parties as second-best compromises would appear to indicate that conversations that would challenge important mental prisons are becoming thinkable.

This sort of debate is unlikely to be initiated as long as the terrain is quasifully occupied by beneficiaries, and unabashedly compassionate journalists and experts. These three groups have little tolerance for ambiguity: they thrive on self-righteousness and black-and-white problem definitions and solutions. These groups have made public administration an inhabitable terrain because of their doctrinaire positions. Indeed, they would no more try to tackle normative questions like the workings of the second invisible hand than allow a compromise response to be entertained as plausible – a solution that would be regarded as a betrayal of their creed, even though such a compromise might be politically desirable.

The only hope might be a return of politics in public administration. This might be the only way to de-fundamentalize the debates about the failures of the two invisible hands. Some wise observers are already calling for a drift in this direction.[26] But there may be no shortcut except through a revolution in the mind first – a revolution that would recognize the legitimate existence of many different *ordres de grandeur,* or legitimate reference points, and the need to find an appropriate blending of perspectives based on the recognition of each party's views as legitimate to a degree. This would delegitimize clinging to extreme ideological positions, and would allow a reasonable code of honour to emerge that would stand somewhere on the continuum – between living on welfare being regarded as dishonourable, to its being crystallized as a fundamental right and honourable

[26]Michael W. Spicer. 2010. *In Defense of Politics in Public Administration – A Value Pluralist Perspective.* Tuscaloosa, AL: The University of Alabama Press.

entitlement. Any negotiated position on this continuum might be regarded as tolerable and honourable, but only temporarily, and contingently – depending on circumstances.

Modest general propositions

The governance of equability must start with the demythologization of the notions of equality and of egalitarianism.

This is a work that has been underway for quite a while in the tradition of the indictment initiated by Tocqueville. Its has been done in different ways: first, through frontal attacks by Harry Frankfurt or John Kekes among others,[27] on the very meaningfulness of such ideals; second, through a probing of the toxic, deleterious and violence-generating impact of the pursuit of such ideals,[28] and third, through finessing all sorts of attenuation of the basal notions of equality and egalitarianism via the deconstruction of its polysemic nature, the affirmation of necessary trade-offs with many other valuable purposes, and the denunciation of undue reliance on *ex post* relative incomes and resources, rather than on the more fundamental insufficiencies of basic capabilities, ascertained *ex ante*.[29]

The net results of these efforts may have been intellectually powerful, but they have done little to minimize the *dominium* of equality and egalitarianism in the lifeworld. The observations of Tocqueville remain extraordinarily salient in the 21st century: envy remains a phenomenal force, and still carries the day. The dynamics of the psycho-social underground remains the main driver that ensures that egalitarianism remains a constant reference.

---

[27] Harry G. Frankfurt. 1987. "Equality as a Moral Ideal," *Ethics*, 98(1): 21-43; John Kekes, 2003, *op. cit.*

[28] Paul Laurent and Gilles Paquet. 1998. *Epistémologie et économie de la relation – coordination et gouvernance distribuée*. Paris/Lyon, FR: Vrin, chapter 12; Bruno Lussato. 1989. *Le défi culturel*. Paris, FR: Nathan.

[29] Amartya Sen. 1995. *Inequality Reexamined*. Oxford, UK: Oxford University Press.

Consequently, it will be a Herculean job to dislodge this passion for equality from its dominant position in the culture, despite all the costs generated by this stance. An epistemological coup based on a crippled epistemology is responsible for this dominance, and nothing less than another epistemological coup will succeed in slaughtering this sacred cow.

The governance of equability must be rooted in sufficiency and respected as a way to diffuse envy and contain redistribution.

To topple egalitarianism, it is necessary to make it unpalatable and dishonourable, but this is not sufficient. It is also important to tame the envy at the source of this drive, and to contain redistribution as a futile response to the egalitarian drive.

On the envy front, G.M. Foster has examined in detail various cultural forms used by persons who either fear the envy of others, or fear that they may be suspected of envy.[30] These take a variety of forms: from concealment, denial and sharing (symbolic or real) in the first instance, to reassurance and withdrawal in the second instance. But there is also a gamut of institutional devices to reduce envy and contain violence: redistributive mechanisms, but also diverse forms of encapsulation and segregation, designed to mark boundaries between groups.

On the redistribution side, the containment could come from an alternative to the doctrine of equality – the *doctrine of sufficiency* – the idea that what is important from a moral point of view is not that everyone should have the same, but that each should have enough. Frankfurt has developed this alternative more fully in a 1997 paper.[31] He argues that there is no necessary connection between having a low social position and having a low quality of life. Treating persons with respect entails dealing with them impartially and without arbitrariness. One should not confuse being treated disrespectfully with being treated unequally. And if greater equality is to be regarded

---

[30] G.M. Foster. 1972. "The Anatomy of Envy: A Study of Symbolic Behavior," *Current Anthropology*, 13(2): 165-186.

[31] Harry Frankfurt. 1997. "Equality and Respect," *Social Research*, 64(1): 3-15.

as desirable, it should be only because it facilitates the pursuit of other socially desirable aims, not because one regards envy as warranting it. The governance of equability must not be allowed to fall prey to the infernal logic of position and envy.[32]

The governance of equability must establish why equability and equability of what, and allow some inequalities in order to avoid worse ones.

Equability would therefore focus on sufficiency rather than on equality and egalitarianism. This does not make it easier to determine what is sufficient, and what sort of inequalities might be undesirable for other socially desirable aims, but the focus and intent are different: as Frankfurt would put it, the focus is on respect and sufficiency, not on giving a dominant place to envy and equality of outcomes in whatever form.

This does not deny that a significant degree of inequality may be of relevance in the pursuit of other desirable aims, and that corrections to these situations must depend on circumstances. For instance, if there is an agent responsible for a discrepancy-generating inequality of condition because the agent has failed to treat each person with respect, it may be objectionable, not because of inequality of outcome, but because of the lack of respect.

This leads to certain pragmatism in recognizing that there are different *ordres de grandeurs* that one must blend in defining regimes of engagement, that the governance of equability must therefore gauge the desirability of many social aims, and that the way of defining unacceptable inequalities depends not on the degree of envy that it fuels (which in itself is not a defendable basis for anything)[33] but on the extent or degree to which such a state of affairs may impair the pursuit of other legitimate social aims.

---

[32] Paul Dumouchel and Jean-Pierre Dupuy. 1979. *L'enfer des choses*. Paris, FR: Éditions du Seuil.

[33] It is astounding to hear some egalitarian like Ronald Dworkin indulge in speculation about the "envy test" of the ideal distribution – one that would leave no one envious of any other person – and that he proposes therefore to elevate the vice of envy to the role of moral standard. See John Kekes critical comments on that position in J. Kekes, 2003, *op.cit.*, 70ff.

This leads to the conclusion that the denunciation of inequality *per se*, and the elevation of egalitarianism to the role of dominant value is illegitimate and unwarranted. Consequently, redistributive policies aimed at taming the destructiveness of envy may have been used unwisely and imprudently. Such imprudence may be particularly toxic when the dynamics triggered by such devices not only interfere with the effective working of the first invisible hand – that of the market – but also the second one – morality. Often, in this latter case, redistribution generates entitlements and changes in belief systems that are fairly difficult to reverse once the common public culture has been tainted.

The outcome of this sort of logic becomes unpalatable and objectionable when a society elicits a culture that edicts that if some resource (however much in excess of the sufficiency level it might be) cannot be made available to all, it should be denied to the one person who can afford it. This is only one step away from the Harrison Bergeron world of Kurt Vonnegut Jr. where, in the name of egalitarianism, one systematically cripples the higher capabilities of superior individuals (by the stronger being forced to carry a load on their shoulders to slow them down, or the brighter ones being equipped with electrodes to ensure that noise bombardment will impair their thinking), all in the name of equalizing down everyone.[34]

Michael Sandel somewhat flippantly discards such a *dérapage* on the grounds that defenders of equality like John Rawls do not wish to emasculate capabilities, but only to redistribute the proceeds from superior abilities.[35] But radical egalitarianism, fueled by envy, is not so tolerant. It argues that if one cannot get access to a certain service, others should be denied it. This is the argument against the so-called two-tiered health care system.

[34] Kurt Vonnegut Jr. 1998. "Harrison Bergeron" in *Welcome to the Monkey House*. New York, NY: Dell.

[35] Michael Sandel. 2009. *Justice – What's the Right Thing to Do?* New York, NY: Farrar, Straus and Giroux, chapter 6.

Conclusion

An entirely new useful research program might be focused on gauging the corridor of wise use of mechanisms to tame envy in our plural and complex world, taking into account that the use of mechanisms has the potential of influencing the moral/ethical underground. This terrain has been shunned by social scientists and has remained largely colonized by fundamentalists and ideologues.

In the case of limited redistribution through time over the cycle, it would appear that economists have been able to regain some hold on this terrain, and to establish fairly well the conditions of success for limited redistribution. When redistribution goes further and encroaches on the system of beliefs and the common public culture, this is *terra incognita*.

| Diversity

"Diversity ... is a watered down,
misguided ideal ... like fraternity lite."
Raymond D. Boisvert

Introduction

Diversity is an opaque and ideologically loaded word, that has been used as a convenient label to connote very different realities, and to underpin quite different action programs.

For some, diversity has been used as a picturesque word to describe the outcome of the great shuffle of population that has led to much more commingling of different groups in many regions of the world, as a result of the reduction of transportation costs and the lowering of territorial border walls. The word also connotes the objective pursued by some countries (either wittingly or unwittingly) to increase such inter-cultural migrations in an effort to recalibrate the age distribution in an ageing country, or to get access to a higher level of creativity and innovation through the cross-pollination of different frames of reference. Thirdly, the word has also been used to characterize, in a clinical fashion, the plight of countries torn apart, or perceived as losing their souls, as a result of either an unwelcome co-habitation of deeply different and hostile groups within the same territory, or of an unbridled invasion of external groups getting established as agents of subversion in the host society and generating fractiousness and factions. In this latter case, diversity implies social friction and higher costs of transaction.

This chapter attempts to clarify the basic underlying issues hidden behind the label of diversity, and to forge the tools necessary for effective governance of diversity.

The issue domain: a few stylized facts

First, variety is a crucial factor in the development of complex systems, but that does not mean that maximum variety is optimum variety. There has to be a balance between the sort of effervescence that accompanies variety and generates novelty, and the need for some basic stability, if efficient social learning and creative adaptation are to ensue.

Second, in the past, diversity was a matter of accident, but globalization has accentuated the intermingling of populations, and most societies have become more or less poly-ethnic, multilingual, etc. Some societies have been disconcerted by such trends, while others have embraced it as a desirable goal. Still, it is not clear what diversity really means. Is it diversity of agents, of traits, of values, of interests? And how much of it is too much?

Third, variety, like any 'social chemical', cannot be examined in isolation, for it interacts with other social chemicals. For instance, there has been an extraordinary growth of symbolic group recognition as a result of the Charter of Rights, and other such developments. In a welfare state environment, this sort of phenomenon has quickly transformed what was a secular custom of hospitality into what is now regarded as a system of rights and entitlements for asylum seekers in the host society. It has meant that symbolic recognition has not been a substitute for material gratification, but a multiplier of such entitlements, commanded by the fraudulent idea of an obligation to indiscriminate altruism. This has had exponential effects, since diversity seemingly has legitimized unbounded demands (financial and others) on the state of the host society.[1]

Fourth, variety appears to be perceived as undermining other social characteristics such as belonging, identification, commitment, etc. Indeed, it is widely presumed that there may be a trade-off between these desirable features of the social fabric and the variety-cum-diversity features. Many deny that there are such trade-offs, but most would admit that diversity is celebrated only as long as these other features are not under threat, especially as the result of an abrupt increase in diversity, even in Canada.[2] If and when diversity requirements appear unbounded (i.e., as in the case of calls for "bend-over-backwards gestures of accommodation"),[3] there is a slip in support, although it may not always dare to show its face.

Fifth, there is great confusion about the complex relationships linking social capital, social cohesion and diversity. Social cohesion has been used too often as a proxy for uniformity, and egalitarian actions have therefore been propounded as the source of social cohesion/uniformity. In fact, the creation of social capital as a label for civic solidarity, organized reciprocity, social networks, etc. – all based on trust – also emerges from conflict, since social learning is enhanced by contrasted perspectives.

Sixth, we are confronted with a major problem of vocabulary. We do not have a language of problem definition that is satisfactory to deal with diversity and pluralism. Too many words – like diversity, identity, belonging, etc. – stand in the way of a meaningful dialogue and limit our analyses by setting multiple traps, of which political correctness is probably the most dangerous one. It has become impossible

---

[1] Ed West. 2011. "Why we need to start discriminating again," *Telegraph Blog*, December 22.

[2] Even those who deny the importance of such trade-offs admit, albeit in a particularly contrived way, that "particular forms of recognition erode particular forms of redistribution." Keith G. Banting. 2007. "Canada as Counter Narrative," *www.optimumonline.ca*, 37(3): 2-15.

[3] Joseph Heath. 2013. "How to avoid the next turban controversy," *Ottawa Citizen*, June 18, A13.

to raise questions about any of these icons (of which diversity is one) without being accused of bigotry.

Seventh, in Canada, one of the most important additions to this complex phenomenon has been the deliberate policy choice by political authorities over the last decades to increase diversity. This has become the main driver of the immigration regime over the last while.[4]

These considerations do not claim to present an exhaustive review of the issue domain, but they broadly define the problem area.[5]

The notion of *governance of diversity* (in the sense of the intentional use of instruments to ascertain how much diversity is too much, and to ensure that such a threshold is respected) has come to be regarded in certain progressive circles as politically incorrect and even as illegitimate. For these critics, diversity would seem not to be a matter of choice, but a matter of fate. For them, refusing to govern the diversity interface would appear to be blessed with the name of virtue, while any effort at attempting to manage the diversity of a society is perceived as a violation of the over-riding principle of indiscriminate compassion, and is readily chastised as a sign of latent fascism. This sort of mindlessness refuses to probe the costs/benefits of embracing more diversity. It makes a surprising double act of faith: first, that diversity is a primary good, and an unmitigated blessing for Canada, and, second, that Canadians have supposedly reached a consensus on this commitment to diversity as a Canada brand, and have been persuaded to stand by with great pride and without a scintilla of concern for its consequences.

My view is in sharp contrast to this bizarre dogmatism. I reckon that a wiser and more robust governance of diversity

---

[4] See the critical evaluation of an official ceremonial presentation of the philosophy of diversity by the Government of Canada by Deborah Carson Tunis in Gilles Paquet. 2012. *Moderato Cantabile: Toward Principled Governance for Canada's Immigration Regime*. Ottawa, ON: Invenire, 85ff.

[5] For a more extensive review of the various dimensions of this problem area, see Gilles Paquet. 2008. *Deep Cultural Diversity – A Governance Challenge*. Ottawa, ON: The University of Ottawa Press.

is a central challenge in *all* pluralistic societies, and that no responsible society can accept being shaped by unchecked faceless external forces, nor can they embrace this sort of situation uncritically.

Moreover, there are reasons to believe that the foundations of the new philosophy of mass immigration and unbounded diversity are not only highly questionable, but also grossly misrepresented when being referred to as the so-called *Canadian consensus*. I would prefer to characterize the nexus of diversity-driven immigration and multiculturalism policies as much more the result of brainwashing and manufactured consent than the outcome of a genuine reasoned organic judgment of the citizenry.

The manufactured Canadian consensus

Up to the last decades of the 20th century, Canada's policy was to encourage immigration and diversity to the extent that it was within the *absorptive capacity* of the country – a shorthand way of taking into account the broader context.[6] This meant that the policy was shaped by a need to ensure that the benefits would outweigh the costs – economic, social, political, cultural, etc. This was slowly abandoned in the final decades of the last century and replaced, in the last 20 years, by a philosophy of mass immigration, explicitly geared to promote diversity as the most important primary good.

This myopic perspective side-swiped carrying capacity as a meaningful economic, psycho-social, political, cultural and moral concept and, therefore, irresponsibly occluded all the external costs of diversity in time and space. A mix of electoralism-inspired lobbying of the immigrant communities, of a superficial self-righteous indiscriminate compassion, and of willful blindness to the foundations of our liberal

---

[6] The notion of carrying capacity has been used by Garrett Hardin to connote the broader context that enables the socio-economy to thrive by remaining within certain limits, or a certain corridor, defined by the social, political, cultural, and moral principles and rules that allow the socio-economy to thrive. See Garrett Hardin. 1976. "Carrying Capacity as an Ethical Concept," *Soundings*, 59, 120-137.

democracy has been skillfully packaged into an amalgam that has been immunized against criticism by a populist veneer, and a melange of emotion and sophistry.

This long drift began with the 1971 proclamation by Pierre Elliott Trudeau that announced the intention of the Canadian government of the day to launch a new Canadian strategy: a more liberal immigration policy and a commitment to multiculturalism. The most fascinating aspect of what ensued is the manner in which this proclaimed strategy acquired intellectual respectability by being subtly theorized, and not so subtly 'judiciarized', before becoming the substance of a politically correct reference point for an unsuspecting, progressively minded populace.

On the conceptual front, a first foundational cornerstone came from John W. Berry's "multicultural assumption"[7] that, simply stated, asserts that only those people who feel secure about their own cultural identity can accept those who are different, and integrate easily in a new context. This assumption was developed as a foundational belief in Canada. This led to the second foundation stone: an extraordinary flourishing of the 'recognition industry' that contends that it is only through the recognition of cultural rights of "others" – be they First Nations, newcomers, etc. – that one can make them feel secure and hope to develop the basis of a workable integration and effective co-habitation. The argumentation of Taylor and Kymlicka made recognition and recognition rights a cornerstone of their defence of multiculturalism. Indeed, in both cases, what was produced was a philosophical basis for a multicultural strategy that was then advertised and promoted around the world as a philosopher's stone.[8]

On the legal front, the folkloric dimensions of the first wave of multiculturalism gave way to ever more formal, if

---

[7] John W. Berry, Rudolf Kalin and Donald M. Taylor. 1977. *Multiculturalism and Ethnic Attitudes in Canada*. Ottawa, ON: Supply and Services Canada.

[8] Will Kymlicka. 1989. *Liberalism, Community and Culture*. Oxford, UK: Oxford University Press; Charles Taylor. 1992. *Multiculturalism and the Politics of Recognition*. Princeton, NJ: Princeton University Press.

cautiously worded, engagements that stimulated a hardening of inter-cultural frontiers, and an inflation of the demands for cultural rights and entitlements. The rights revolution paved the way to minority rights recognition, and the 1971 proclamation became a national policy. This was crystallized most firmly in Article 27 of the Charter of Rights and Freedoms of 1982.

This series of events completely transformed the perception of immigration: between 1986 and 1993, the number of economic immigrants shifted from around 100,000 to something around 250,000, and remained there for the following decades, while, surprisingly, between 1993 and 2003, the Environics public opinion polls response to the question "is there too much immigration?" elicited a complete reversal – two thirds of respondents responding "yes" in 1993, and only one third in 2003. What Berry-Taylor-Kymlicka theorized would appear to have become the new gospel.

The main point in contention is whether this reversal is mainly ascribable to the normal organic evolution of public opinion (echoing rapid changes in underlying reference points, or concerns or opinions, despite the steady flow of scientific studies showing that mass immigration was doing little to promote economic growth, or to correct the demographic age structure), or to disinformation and brainwashing.[9]

First of all, existing research on the motivations at work and the process of formation of public opinion on matters of immigration shows them to be complex. But it would appear that (net of all other factors), it is the *so-called symbolic-political dimension* (reflecting the dominant national discourse in Canada) that has the most important impact. The beliefs about

---

[9] Jeffrey G. Reitz. 2011. *Pro-Immigration Canada – Social and Economic Roots of Popular Views*. Montreal, QC: Institute for Research on Public Policy (IRPP). IRPP would appear to presume that these 'popular views' are an exact reflection of underlying social values. This is an extraordinary presumption, for values do not usually change as dramatically and fundamentally in just a few years. It would appear more reasonable to presume that there is no such virgin birth of public opinion, and that, in the case of immigration in particular, there may be reason to believe that the popular views have been significantly shaped by disinformation and propaganda.

the positive or negative impact of immigration on the nation, or the like, are seen as a major determinant of the choice for expansion or restriction of immigration.[10]

Those research results are crucial, for they underline the importance of the efforts to manufacture a dominant national discourse by a clerisy of groups with an interest in immigration expansion. It is less the personal circumstances of particular individuals than the overall belief in a certain national rationale that appears to be echoed in opinion polls.

Persuading the population that high-levels of immigration are a significant source of economic growth and welfare-enhancement for the country, and that they will contribute to rebalancing the age structure of the population (and thereby help to sustain the financial viability of the welfare state for an ageing Canadian population) has had considerable force in determining the response to questions about the expansion or restriction of immigration levels. These propositions have been repeated by Canadian officials and academics over the last 20 years despite the fact that numerous studies have shown them to be empirically indefensible.[11]

As a result, over the last 20 years, and regardless of the socio-economic conditions, the level of the flow of new immigrants has been raised, and suggestions to tighten the selection criteria – even those recommended by the Immigration Legislative Review – were successfully opposed by immigration activists, immigrant service organizations and the major political parties. This situation continued during the May 2011 federal election campaign, where all parties promised immigration levels higher than the 2010 levels – when 280,000 immigrants had been received – at a time when Canada had just lost close to half a million full-time jobs because of the recession: all because 80 percent of Canadians

---

[10] Jessica Fortin and Peter John Loewen. 2004. "Prejudice and Asymmetrical Opinion Structures: Public Opinion Toward Immigration in Canada," paper presented at the Annual Meeting of the Canadian Political Science Association at the University of Winnipeg, Winnipeg, MB, June 3.

[11] See Gilles Paquet. 2012. *Moderato Cantabile: Toward Principled Governance for Canada's Immigration Regime*. Ottawa: ON: Invenire.

polled had clearly been led to believe (falsely) that high levels of immigration generate economic growth and would correct the demographic imbalance.

These false beliefs were drummed into the Canadian consciousness, and since this is a debate with a certain degree of technical complexity, Canadian citizens have not necessarily invested the requisite time to be able to appreciate the arguments. They have relied on the apparent consensus of opinion-moulders: a certain disinformation by politicians and their consorts.

This disinformation became even more strident more recently because the electoral stakes had become higher. By this time, 20 percent of the Canadian population was foreign-born, and in the case of Toronto and Vancouver, the proportion was close to 50 and 40 percent, respectively. Among the major political parties, it was a case of which one would sound more pro-immigration, and there was implicit collusion among them to prevent any serious discussion of any evidence that seemed to suggest action to the contrary.

Second, it is not clear that this coalition of disinformers would have been anything like as successful as it has been, were it not for the aggressive way in which the philosophy of multiculturalism was bolstered by the Charter of Rights of 1982. This began to bear fruit in the 1980s (the Singh case) when it was argued, invoking the Charter, that once a newcomer put his foot on Canadian soil (legally or not), he could claim entitlement to all the rights of Canadians, except the right to vote. This contention was supported by the Supreme Court of Canada, and as a matter of consequence, Canada lost control of her borders. The Mulroney government could not persuade itself to invoke the notwithstanding clause to defer the application of the decision of the Supreme Court of Canada. Charter activism had already given a new wind to multiculturalism.

This movement came to full maturity in the 1990s, and was accompanied by an extraordinary effort to propagandize and celebrate multiculturalism, and to theorize it as not only progressive and changing the very nature of the social game (and therefore of Canadian identity), but also as a model for the rest of the world.

It is not so much that the books of Charles Taylor and Will Kymlicka triggered the movement: they simply echoed the very active multiculturalist propaganda that had permeated *le pouvoir social* in Canada[12] and theorized it, thereby giving legitimacy to the on-going transformation of the social norms. Indeed, this propagandizing was aimed at making multiculturalism a source of national pride – unity in diversity became the mantra – and a subject of some naïve sort of exultation. The full implications of this leap of faith may not have been understood by the host population, but they were fully grasped as a powerful lever by the newcomers.

This period can be reasonably referred to as one where the Canadian identity was surreptitiously transformed, where the reference points were modified, and where a new ethos came to be dramatically redefined in terms of new truths. Not only were new ideals and norms being brandished, but these new ideals were also articulated in a language of rights and became immunized from any criticism by their Charter base.[13]

Both as a result of a change in the composition of the population and of a mix of disinformation and propaganda to promote the so-called Canadian way, diversity for the sake of diversity became an absolute good and aggressive pursuit of such a good – a sign of moral superiority. It has come to

---

[12] Raymond Boudon. 2005. *Tocqueville aujourd'hui*. Paris, FR: Odile Jacob, p. 167-175. What Tocqueville called *le pouvoir social* connotes the mechanisms through which, on certain topics or issues, a dominant view (however ill-founded it may be) comes to prevail, and to become a dominant view in the face of which even substantive criticism is impotent. In the case of multiculturalism, the chorus of interest groups effectively presented it as 'progressive' and therefore desirable. Eventually, such a view becomes a sort of conventional wisdom. This has led to a growing reluctance to challenge this iconic issue, to the point where anyone doing so faced various forms of censorship.

[13] For a general discussion of the ways in which people and organizations may manipulate categories, norms and ideals, see George A. Akerlof and Rachel E. Kranton. 2010. *Identity Economics*. Princeton, NJ: Princeton University Press, 124ff.

dominate the national discourse. Moreover, any opposition to these beliefs met with a certain amount of social odium. So it is misleading to speak of a consensus that would have emerged organically. It is because of deception that Canadian citizens support that policy.

Canadians have been re-programmed. Therefore, it is now regarded as politically incorrect to hold the views they held in the 1980s, and so these views are no longer revealed. Therefore, one may question the meaningfulness of what is labelled the *Canadian consensus* on such issues as recorded in polls. What the polls are harvesting are the results generated by a mix of disinformation and propaganda sown over the previous few decades.

Consequently, at a time when around the world there is much reflection on the limits to the multicultural strategy adopted by Canada,[14] there is very little debate about these issues in Canada itself. Canadians seem to have slipped into groupthink, into a sort of politically correct mental prison. And both the intelligentsia and the media work collaboratively to guard this prison!

Some reviewers of this manuscript have found some of my criticisms of the Canadian intelligentsia and media as agents of disinformation and propagandizing in the diversity file somewhat harsh. To illustrate the routine way in which the orthodox view is propagandized, and any countering point of view is suppressed, I append, at the end of this chapter, an op-ed piece I sent to the *Ottawa Citizen* on June 19, 2013, in response to an article by Joseph Heath published on June 18, 2013 in the newspaper. This response was not published as could be expected. Indeed the only reaction to Heath's paper that was published was a very supportive view from an immigration lawyer damning Quebec's identity anxiety as an impediment to "the march of history" – defined by the need of immigration and the concept of multiculturalism.

This is the case in the editorial pages of a newspaper that has occasionally allowed unorthodox views about diversity

---

[14] Ed West. 2013. *The Diversity Illusion*. London, UK: Gibson Square.

to be aired by its columnists at least. This is most certainly not the case in the *Toronto Star* or the *Globe & Mail* where zealotry prevails everywhere in the diversity file.

A fragile social fabric and its dilemmas

There have been many studies on the economic costs of the new philosophy of mass immigration and diversity. But the social and cultural costs associated with the erosion of the country's social fabric may be even more important and more irreversible than has been presumed. The reason is simple. Such studies are particularly complex, and standard indicators of fairness, trust or belonging are not readily available and reliable, so very few social scientists are adventurous enough to focus their studies in this direction.

An interesting exception is the 2004 study by Raymond Breton and colleagues.[15] They have more or less psychoanalyzed the Canadian population by mining survey data. Their work reveals a fragile social fabric in Canada and some disquieting trends: trust, recognition and perception of fairness are in decline. This entails an erosion of social relations, a decline in the sense of belonging, and a decrease in the contributions to communal life.

Breton et al. are extraordinarily cautious when it comes to explaining the sources and causes of these fragilities in the social fabric, but they point to the fact that increased diversity is part of the nexus of forces generating social fragmentation and the erosion of social capital.

Despite the caution of the Breton study from which one might derive some sense that diversity may not be the central force at work, some other studies have been skirting the edge of this issue domain, raising two social dilemmas: are there deep tensions at work in Canada between heterogeneity and redistribution, and between recognition and redistribution?

---

[15] Raymond Breton et al. 2004. *A Fragile Social Fabric? Fairness, Trust and Commitment in Canada.* Montreal, QC and Kingston, ON: McGill-Queen's University Press.

Keith Banting has dealt with these questions.[16] On the basis of the empirical work done by a pan-Canadian research team, Banting was able to conclude that "there is no evidence ... that countries with large immigrant populations have greater difficulty in sustaining and enhancing their historic welfare commitments. But large increases in the foreign-born population do seem to matter."[17] As for the second, and much more difficult question (as to whether explicit recognition policies like official multiculturalism tend to weaken redistribution), there seems to be no support for it as a bald claim, but an admission that "there are more localized circumstances where particular forms of recognition erode particular forms of redistribution."[18]

This sort of work reached a climax in the summer of 2007 with the publication of Robert Putnam's *E Pluribus Unum*.[19] This paper, based on a study of over 30,000 people and over 40 communities across America, comes to the clear conclusion that, after normalizing the data to standardize for all sorts of extraneous factors, more diversity means lower social capital, and that diversity, at least in the short run, seems to entail less social cohesion – less volunteer work, less charity, less voting, less involvement, less belief that the citizen can make a difference.

Given the time lags that might be involved in the generation and disappearance of such tensions, the empirical work on these difficult questions leaves these questions unresolved in any definitive way for the long run.

Even though the empirical work does not clearly robustly support the hypothesis that there is some tension and trade-off between recognition and solidarity (as measured by redistribution), it is quite difficult to believe – given the extraordinary resistance to any symbolic recognition (like distinct society) and the general apprehension generated

[16] Keith G. Banting, 2007, *op.cit.*

[17] *Ibid.*, p. 7.

[18] *Ibid.*, p. 10.

[19] Robert D. Putnam. 2007. "*E Pluribus Unum*: Diversity and Community in the 21st Century," *Scandinavian Political Studies*, 30(2): 137-174.

by the slogan "different but equal" – that an increase in symbolic recognition, and therefore in separateness, does not reduce solidarity.

Indeed, much anecdotal evidence would appear to reveal that the sharper and the more publicly celebrated the symbolic recognition of separateness (as in the case of French Canadians and the Aboriginals), the more the sense of belonging and trust is eroded. One can choose to ascribe such antagonism to history, but it is simplistic to discard separateness as a root cause. And it is clear that if recognition and separateness are clearly encouraged by a multicultural approach, it can only generate a weakening of the social fabric over the long haul. How can the determination to remain apart generate anything different despite what the multiple regressions suggest?

The worst aspect of the formalization and 'judiciarization' of these differences that the multiculturalism approach encourages is that it fosters a certain civic *malaise* as these phenomena shape a certain way for minorities and immigrant groups to think about their problem, to bet on their differences, to play the 'humiliation card', and to demand greater equalization.

A primer on the governance of diversity

The governance of diversity entails the harnessing of the forces at work in defining the desirable degree of balkanization and *métissage* involved in the fabric of an efficient and decent society, and the optimal speed or rate at which such drifts should be allowed to proceed. For true variety does not simply mean additive layers or groups of individuals living in totally separate worlds as in a quilt. Such patchwork generates apartheid societies that are neither plural nor diverse in the true sense. If the degree of interaction between groups cannot be zero, it may vary greatly, according to the different regimes in place, and may be more or less tolerable or viable depending on circumstances. Again, the rate at which these interactions are modified may also be non-optimal.

A regime is a set of explicit or implicit principles, norms, rules, behaviour patterns, arrangements, decision-making procedures, and institutions around which actor expectations converge. It is neither orderly nor systematic, but reveals some internal consistency and technical proficiency.

The mechanisms or technologies of collaboration are guideposts, moral contracts, conventions and the like, that are the core of the regimes. They are not only the processes through which coordination occurs, but the ways in which the limits beyond which one is not allowed to proceed are implicitly defined.

De facto, the set of rules in good currency and generally acknowledged are defining limits, very much like the speed limit on the road implicitly spells out what is regarded as the tolerable death toll on our roads. But there is often a considerable gap between the rules and the state of mind of the population. Rules are defined in the light of sanctimonious discourses that do not always take into account the unintended consequences of what would appear on the surface as reasonable rules.

Good governance entails a process of guiding that is transparent, inclusive, participative and fairly effective, through the crafting of mechanisms in keeping with the dominant logic of the regime, and likely to generate a capacity to transform as circumstances change.

Contrat de citoyenneté

The central challenge is to use the *contrat de citoyenneté* as a terrain to construct the terms of integration, and identify the limits to diversity.

Canadians, as individuals, are inclined to be both much more demanding than Canadian officials in their definition of citizenship, and to be much more willing than bureaucrats and politicians to craft *de facto* workable terms of integration. They define it not only in terms of a bundle of rights and liberties, but also in terms of responsibilities, attitudes and identities.

But public officials (for whom expediency is the dominant value) claim to have no concern about defining for newcomers any such set of expectations about the terms of integration on the ground that one cannot ask anything from newcomers that one does not require explicitly from native born. Making any additional demands of newcomers is automatically branded as intolerance, chauvinism or racism.

As a matter of consequence, officials are not much concerned with ensuring that newcomers are provided with the requisite help to make them capable of participating fully in the host society, and feel that they have no legitimate basis to refuse to modify the Canadian ways in response to requests by newcomers' claim that such ways constitute a discriminatory stance against them.

The result is not only a lack of debate in Canada (except, of late, in Quebec) about the limits to tolerance and diversity, but a natural drift, as the jurisprudence cranks out case after case, towards a refusal in official circles to recognize that there are any limits to diversity.

This is no longer pluralism, but a leap of faith that if some form of limits prove necessary, it will emerge organically. It is quite a gamble, since the required terms of integration are, in fact, likely to emerge only from a continuous renegotiation as the expectations and environments change, and from an explicit statement of rights and responsibilities; but it will also emerge out of the limits to tolerance of the host society, and of the obligations this will entail for the newcomers to adapt somewhat. Canadian leaders refuse to confront this challenge.

The present refusal by Canadian officials to engage in an exercise of definition of terms of integration is understandable, but not inconsequential. The lack of a clear notion of the responsibilities of citizenship can only lead to a great fuzziness in the definition of the limits of tolerance. More than any other factor, the very reluctance of the Canadian government to foster debates leading to a clear articulation of what the guideposts are in this fuzzy land is probably the main source of concern for those who favour tighter controls on immigration in Canada.

The danger of this unwillingness to establish clear conditions of admission, and terms of integration, is that it has allowed extreme forms of the erosion of trust, as significant groups have found it opportune to take advantage of the

Canadian benefits, without accepting any of the obligations that constitute the flip side of this moral contract of citizenship. As a result of such abuses,[20] this can only lead in the longer run to action generating greater exclusion than would otherwise be desirable, and both old and new Canadians are consequently bound to be worse off.

Intermediate cosmopolitanism as the way out

Instead of starting from a position that emphasizes inherent differences, separate status, fractured lines and some 'recognized' reified identity (with the consequent challenges of having to find ways to overcome these differences, both inherited and nurtured – as multiculturalism suggests), one might want to build on a loose notion of cosmopolitanism. This connotes a vague concept of worldliness and a readiness to accept differences (however profound) as not so important, and to accept living with largely un-acclimatized evolving groups (with the consequence that a civil society-based regime might allow us to economize on all those nations-cum-*ethnies*-based integrative constructs that have, up to now, proved beyond our reach).

Cosmopolitanism

Cosmopolitanism is a tainted word. It has been used by many to suggest quite different realities – from the way of life of the successful, who cut the links to their original community to partake in the exclusive network of the supranational elite, to the lifestyle of those vagrants not bound to any country and characterized by a certain rootlessness and footlooseness as they move around the world. This is a particularly cavalier and dismissive way of dealing with what is, in fact, an alternative way to describe 'the other.'

[20] A recent example is the refusal by Chiheb Esseghaier (a man accused of having conspired to create the derailment of a VIA train) to be judged on the basis of the Canadian Criminal Code, thereby revealing that some newcomers even refuse to abide by the rule of law when coming to Canada (*Radio-Canada*, June 22, 2013).

K.A. Appiah has rehabilitated the concept by defining it as a meshing of two strands: the idea of obligations to others, and the idea of taking interest in them and learning from them.[21] The reasonable cosmopolitan relates to the other in a way that is neither utopian (all human beings being treated as equals is both unnatural and unrealistic) nor entirely disconnected (strangers being regarded as of another species is also unacceptable, except to the bigots). Cosmopolitans follow a third way. They presume that "all cultures have enough overlap in their vocabulary of values to begin a conversation."[22] This does not presume that there will be an agreement, but that there will be a conversation. Cosmopolitanism is "connection not through identity but despite difference."[23]

In that sense, cosmopolitanism (the C-approach) is the obverse of multiculturalism, which wishes to establish connection through building stronger separate identity claims, and arguing, as Charles Taylor and others have done for decades, that more robust recognition will make connections easier.

Let us agree from the start that radically strong cosmopolitanism is unreal: the idea that each of us has equal responsibilities to all persons worldwide is utopian. And radically weak cosmopolitanism (boutique cosmopolitanism), based on the most superficial interest in exoticism and the like, is anodyne. But *intermediate cosmopolitanism* is not anodyne and superficial. It asserts that "all persons have a negative duty … toward every human being not to collaborate in imposing an unjust institutional order upon him or her,"[24] and it adds that special, thicker relationships can increase what we feel we owe to closer associates (family, compatriots, etc.) but cannot decrease what we owe everyone else. Intermediate

[21] K. Anthony Appiah. 2006. *Cosmopolitanism – Ethics in a World of Strangers.* New York, NY: Norton, p. xv.

[22] *Ibid.*, p. 57.

[23] *Ibid.*, p. 135.

[24] Thomas W. Pogge. 2002. "Cosmopolitanism: A Defense," *Critical Review of International Social and Political Philosophy,* 5(3): 89.

cosmopolitanism is an interesting reference through which to appraise other strategies to cope with deep cultural diversity, such as multiculturalism. It is important to have such a reference since, without one, no meaningful benchmarking is possible.

Cosmopolitanism as an alternative to multiculturalism
Multiculturalists, *grosso modo*, tend to reify culture and identity somewhat, and are led to call for cultural rights. This leads to an overstatement of differences, and to an inflation of the rights of recognition of these differences. Such a hardening of the boundaries leads to much ethno-political entrepreneurship to reinforce them, and a weakening of citizenship.

Conversely, cosmopolitanism tends to promote a transcultural approach. It emphasizes less the variety of group cultures than the cultural variety of individuals and their multiple and limited identities. Instead of consecrating the 'coexistence of non-communicating vessels', and identity politics, it promotes a mediated solidarity between strangers, based on equal worth of individuals and a high degree of impartiality of treatment (i.e., all claims arising being subject to rules that all can share) – all this emerging from our shared humanity. These presumptions avoid the dangerous trap of those who make the false assumption that just because human beings are born equal, cultures are too.

In fact, as Michael Ignatieff aptly put it, "without this fiction – that human similarity is primary and difference secondary – we are sunk."[25] What must be avoided at all cost is losing sight of the fact that we are individuals, and that we must see each other as such. We must also avoid turning individuals into "carriers of hated group characteristics." John Keane refers to the "new civilians" as those individual bearers of such a basic identity who refuse any primary marker by sole virtue of being a person belonging to a particular group.[26]

---

[25] Michael Ignatieff. 1999. *Warrior's Hour: War and the Modern Conscience.* London, UK: Vintage, p. 70.

[26] John Keane. 1998. *Civil Society.* Cambridge, UK: Polity Press.

The M-approach and the C-approach

One of the key elements brought to light by comparing the M-approach (multiculturalism) to the C-approach (cosmopolitanism) is the fact that the M-approach, very much like assimilationism, assumes bounded and rival majority and minority cultures. It insists on a separate minority existence and, in Canada, on the maintenance and enhancement of that separateness.

The C-approach does not presume that cultures are different, but that individuals partake in a variety of cultures. As a result, the C-approach (1) perceives the M-approach as threatening for citizenship, and (2) paves the way to experiments with forms of true integration via a refurbished notion of citizenship. Indeed, citizenship is seen by the C-approach as a most useful conduit to serve as a cauldron in which both majorities and minorities are transformed. It can therefore be suggested that the drift toward citizenship, as the way in which some countries (the UK, the Netherlands and Australia) are trying to cope with the deep diversity challenge, may well amount to developing some workable new covenant inspired by cosmopolitanism.

This new reference is built on concord, or what Aristotle called *homonoia* – a relationship between people who are not strangers, between whom goodwill is possible, but not friendship: a relationship based on respect for differences. Raymond Boisvert has attempted to capture the result of this sort of exercise. For him, diversity can only be tackled by *fraternization* or what he calls *creolization* – a dynamic process of creative interplay, based on amalgamation, merging and blending.[27] It squarely and resolutely challenges the silo-style co-existence and separateness that the M-approach invites. Whether this alternative approach, based on trust and a capacity to interact with strangers in a positive, limited, but exploratory and learning way, is workable is a legitimate question. It would most certainly appear to hold more promise, and to present less risk than the current M-strategy.

[27] Raymond D. Boisvert. 2005. "Diversity as Fraternity Lite," *Journal of Speculative Philosophy*, 19(2): 120-128.

Two roots to cosmopolitan solidarity

In a fundamental way, we are sent back to the questions raised by Michael Ignatieff in his book, *The Needs of Strangers*, of some 30 years ago.[28] Ignatieff explores ground zero of human obligation to the claims of strangers. He is searching for a language of the good that might answer this question. But he leaves his readers still dissatisfied. Appiah revisited this question, some 20 years later, and attempted to provide a language to deal with it.[29]

Appiah has come up with what he calls a "wishy-washy version of cosmopolitanism,"[30] rooted in two concepts of obligation, drawing on a distinction between morality and ethics. Morality has to do with what we owe to others, and ethics with what sort of life it is good for us to live; morality involves duties to persons with whom one has thin relationships, while ethics involves duties to oneself, and to those with whom one enjoys thick relations.[31] There are complex trade-offs between these normative registers, but it would be unwise to assume that one should always dominate the other.

As Appiah puts it, "moral obligations must discipline ethical ones,"[32] but again there is no absolute. What one is faced with is a series of "imaginary communities" that call for more or less thick relationships, more or less special responsibilities, and more or less partiality. These communities span the territory between perfect strangers and the self and, somewhere along the continuum, the moral becomes ethical or vice-versa.

Whether imaginary communities generate thick or thin relations is an open question. Whether such relationships benefit from being formalized and discussed in the language of rights is also an open question. But these relationships need not be completely theorized and, most of the time, they get resolved in practical ways rather than through agreements

[28] Michael Ignatieff. 1984. *The Needs of Strangers*. New York, NY: Viking.
[29] K. Anthony Appiah. 2005. *The Ethics of Identity*. Princeton, NJ: Princeton University Press.
[30] *Ibid.*, p. 222.
[31] *Ibid.*, p. 230.
[32] *Ibid.*, p. 233.

on basic principles or as embodiment of a general concept. Moreover, the very notion of community may be said to inhabit a much wider range than what comes to mind when one refers to geographical contiguity.

George Saunders' satirical fable of "fluid nations" echoes the fact that imaginary communities are limited only by the resourcefulness of the imagination: men who fish, or persons who make excellent strudel, are communities.[33] Saunders has a field day savaging the arbitrariness of the ways communities sort themselves out, and the absurdity of categorical chauvinism.

What is most paradoxical is the way in which the M-approach has succeeded in bestowing rights and entitlements on some communities, while other equally meaningful communities have failed to acquire any.

Becoming a cosmopolitan

Whatever the attractiveness of the cosmopolitan idea, it has acquired a utopian image in Canada. Cosmopolitan, like liberal, has become a word that connotes ideological stances in the organizational culture. So it is naïve to presume that the market for ideas can operate as a perfect market under such circumstances. The organizational culture operates as a robust filtre. The organizational culture is defined by the ideas, customs and values that have been nurtured or have proven useful over the decades, and continue to be regarded as making up an appropriate appreciative system that is both enabling and limiting. It echoes both a set of readinesses and capacities, and a set of mental constraints or taboos that prevent the system from choosing certain options when faced with unforeseen challenges.

The organizational culture in Canada may be roughly gauged as standing somewhere between the continental European communitarian ethos and the American individualistic ethos (very much like the UK, Australia and the like). Canada is regarded as soft universalist,

---

[33] George Saunders. 2003. "A Survey of the Literature," *The New Yorker*, September 22.

individualistic, somewhat risk-averse, inner-directed, short-term oriented, and biased toward equality.[34] As a result, even though there are no reasons not to experiment with cosmopolitan ways, the soft communitarian mindset has blocked that perspective out.

Multiculturalism and the Charter have been made possible largely because they were mini-*coups d'état*. The population was carried along without really understanding the real impact of these mammoth changes. When special commissions and referenda focused the attention of the citizenry on institutional change (Meech, Charlottetown), risk aversion in the face of significant gambles and a fundamental attachment to 'equality' (even when it was grossly unfair) led to a massive rejection.

This is why so many in Canada and elsewhere are still "closeted cosmopolitans", and why becoming a cosmopolitan will require denouncing many of these mental prisons, battling against tribalism, and "halting the habituated practice of capitulating to the arbitrary glib and specious ends of the labellers and categorizers."[35] Moreover, "to come out" will require a serious questioning of the degree of state centricity of Canadian governance, and of the seductions of egalitarianism in a world that is *de facto* willing to settle for no more than equability.

The journey to transculturalism

It may legitimately be asked how this journey from a clearly flawed multiculturalism strategy (built on emphasizing differences inherited from the past) to a more promising neo-republican strategy of transculturalism (emphasizing forward-looking experimentation and *metissage*) might be best carried out. Suffice it to say that it will not be easy, and that my anticipatory guided tour of the prospective journey is likely to sound immensely politically incorrect.

---

[34] Gilles Paquet. 2009. *Crippling Epistemologies and Governance Failures – A Plea For Experimentalism*. Ottawa, ON: The University of Ottawa Press, chapter 3.
[35] Jason D. Hill. 2000. *Becoming a Cosmopolitan: What It Means to Be a Human Being in the New Millenium*. Oxford, UK: Rowman & Littlefield, 159ff.

In summary, it can be said that Canadians are condemned to a slow evolution from multiculturalism to transculturalism. This is ascribable to some mental prisons in which citizens have been trapped by their politicians over the past 40 years, and to some learning challenges that they will have to overcome.

Dismantling two mental prisons

Over 35 years of cultural programming by the multicultural engine, and the particularly powerful endorsement of this strategy by Article 27 of the Charter in 1982, have had quite an impact on the Canadian way of dealing with deep cultural diversity. Preserving and enhancing inherent differences is the guiding principle in good currency in our multicultural regime. Division and fracture lines are automatically conceded.

Modulating Article 27

For the time being, the multicultural strategy is deeply rooted in the Charter of Rights and Freedoms. Article 27 is like a time bomb, waiting to be used at any time by the Supreme Court to reinforce the intercultural fracture lines in Canada. All sorts of rights have been merrily confounded with the basic conditions of citizenry.[36]

From the irresponsible Singh decision in the 1980s forward, the Supreme Court has redefined citizenship. It has of late taken onto itself the role of dabbling in matters of 'dignity', and it is entirely predictable that it will find it permissible to widen considerably the ambit of Article 27.

Nothing less than a clear statement on this matter by Parliament will do. It might serve to indicate what it will not allow the Supreme Court to do, and state clearly that it intends to use the notwithstanding clause if and when the Supreme Court were to choose to reinforce the fracture lines.

---

[36] Article 27 of the 1982 Canadian Charter of Rights and Freedoms states that it "must be interpreted in a manner consistent with the preservation and enhancement of the multicultural heritage of Canadians."

Toning down egalitarianism

The extraordinary ideological power of egalitarianism, and of the language of rights, has been mentioned in the last chapter. This ideological bent is even more toxic when it is applied to cultures. Especially after some 40 years of multicultural boosterism, almost entirely based on the presumption that all cultures are equal, it may prove very difficult to persuade Canadians that the sort of identity politics that it has underpinned is not the way.

A whole set of flawed narratives are based on these foundations, and are fuelling *ressentiment* and recrimination. Those who claim to be the defenders of prudence and moderation (and there are many) will have to accept that no progress can be made until this musket is disarmed.

It is part of the conceptual refurbishment that is called for by the transformation of the *Welfare State* into a *Strategic State*, and for the recognition that although citizens are equal in law, this does not mean that cultures are equal, whatever their state of development.

Overcoming learning challenges

Shaking off cognitive dissonance

Much of the essentialism in good currency (be it of the statist, nationalist or other variety) is rooted in an effort to deny deep diversity, and to assume it to be a much more superficial phenomenon than it really is. This leads to a failure to acknowledge the Myrdal cumulative causation mechanism,[37] and to some wishful thinking about all our differences melting away over a few generations.

Integration is seen as likely to emerge organically, and would appear to require no intervention and, most certainly, no effort to put in place a governance regime capable of generating a dynamic and transculturally-oriented *métissage*.

---

[37] Paul Laurent and Gilles Paquet. 1991. "Intercultural Relations: A Myrdal-Tocqueville-Girard Interpretative Schema," *International Political Science Review*, 12(3): 171-183.

This perspective is flawed in two ways. First, what we know about the dynamics of intercultural relations promises much violence in this so-called interim period that not only may last a century or more, but may also leave us with irreversible balkanization and damage to the country. Second, the Panglossian view that integration will take care of itself may lead to a failure to take the action that would promise a less destructive future.[38]

Citizenship redux, moral contracts deployed

Recombinant citizenship and a richness of varied moral contracts are likely to help, but only on the condition that the scope of citizenship is dramatically reduced and the ambit of locally defined moral contracts expanded dramatically.

Only the neo-republicans would appear to have a sufficiently modest notion of citizenship. For them, citizenship is the primary office: citizens are producers of governance. This means that citizenship pertains to the public realm, to the polis, and that it does not require the elimination of differences of standing and power.[39] For them, social rights are not citizen rights,[40] and they stand firm against the trend, beginning with T.H. Marshall, to allow an unbounded extension of rights attached to citizenship. We have shown the sorts of abuses to which it has led.

Citizens need to be competent, and to have the sort of rights required to carry out their duty of governing in the community of fate. They are not agents of identity groups. They can negotiate various particular arrangements for groups as long as, practically, such compromises or accommodations do not create too many new inequalities or conflicts. Pragmatism is the rule.

---

[38] The Jason Kenney era (when Kenney was the Canadian federal minister in charge of the multiculturalism and immigration files (2007-2013)) has been one in which integration has become the main focus of Canadian policy, but it did not fully succeed in counterbalancing decades of neglect on this front.

[39] Herman R. van Gunsteren. 1998. *A Theory of Citizenship – Organizing Plurality in Contemporary, Democracies*. Boulder, CO: Westview Press, 24ff.

[40] *Ibid.*, p. 106.

Emergent social movements may well generate new dynamics by expressing new needs and desires, produce new actors, make questionable what was not previously questioned, and expand the options discussed within the public sphere.[41] In that sense, emergent publics feed the public debate on citizenry. But it would be naïve to be looking for simple consensus. The public in a deeply diverse society is always divided. And the range of arrangements (formal or informal) that different fragments will find workable is quite wide. Practically, this may translate not so much into uniform and homogeneous arrangements but into a variety of diverse accommodations, within a corridor of arrangements regarded as not too politically destabilizing.

This accommodates the agency of persons with multiple and limited identities. As long as the different levels of citizenship are balancing rights and duties, one may be allowed to define the sort of constellation of citizenship arrangements that suits his/her preferences. De facto, such differentiated citizenships exist in many countries. The only difference is that most of the time it is not a matter of choice, but a status imposed on the person for all sorts of reasons. The more reduced the scope of citizenship (as the neo-republican suggests), the more it is rooted in action and practice; and the more the preconditions are not related to action and practice, the less contentious is the notion of differentiated citizenship.

More importantly, this approach might resolve, in a manner that provides for *agency, but with some sense of precedence*, the thorny question of multiple citizenships. Each person would have the choice of balancing rights and responsibilities *ex ante* in a manner that might resolve the conundrum generated by the tension between diversity and solidarity. Differentiated citizenship might provide for *major* and *minor* attachments, and so resolve the problem of *citizenship of convenience*, and the possibility of blithely collecting multiple entitlements (pensions, for instance), while shirking all responsibilities.

[41] Ian H. Angus. 2001. *Emergent Publics – An Essay on Social Movements and Democracy*. Winnipeg, MB: Arbeiter Ring Publishing, 55ff.

This would also free up much of the negotiation space for the development of a multitude of different moral contracts, suitable to local circumstances.

Conclusion

This world in transformation may provide very useful opportunities for intervention.

Some years ago, Hubert Reeves evoked an event of 1942 when forest fires, caused by bombardments in Russia, forced about 1000 horses to jump into the Ladoga Lake to save themselves.[42] Even though there had been a sweep of very cold air over the area in recent days, the water was still liquid. While the horses were swimming toward the other side of the lake, it froze suddenly. The day after, the horses were all ice monuments in the middle of the frozen lake. The explanation of this phenomenon is rather simple. When the drop in temperature is too rapid, water does not have time to congeal into ice, and remains liquid at a temperature below zero. But this water is in a quite unstable state: it can take very little to trigger the process of ice crystallization instantly.

In the first portion of the 21st century, nation-states have been in such an *état de surfusion*. This explains why a revolution of sorts might be quickly effected.

If we are right, it may take much less effort than is anticipated by many to effect such a major reframing as the exploration of the C-approach. What specific factor or event might trigger this mutation is not entirely clear, but it is likely to be the result of an investment in *possibilism* – a deliberate investment in the discovery of paths, however narrow, leading to an outcome that appears to be foreclosed on the basis of probabilistic reasoning alone.[43]

In such a world of *surfusion*, a little disturbance is sufficient. And it may well be that, as Jason Hill put it, "a single solitary effrontery does leave the world changed."[44]

---

[42] Hubert Reeves. 1986. *L'heure de s'enivrer*. Paris, FR: Seuil.

[43] Albert O. Hirschman. 1971. *A Bias for Hope*. New Haven, CT: Yale University Press.

[44] Jason Hill, 2000, *op.cit.*, p. 162.

| Annex

Joseph Heath's Golden Rule[45]

G iven Joseph Heath's earlier debunking of the myth of shared Canadian values,[46] and his lucid appreciation of the importance of the rules and norms of vivre-ensemble – making up the common public culture – to enable all of us to live together in a pluralist society, I would have expected Joseph Heath to question the forthcoming Quebec government proposal of a Charter of Quebec Values, as likely to be illiberal, and to encourage rather negotiating shared rules and norms.[47]

However Joseph Heath uses the Quebec head-gear soccer farce as an occasion to launch a tear-jerking defense of multiculturalism as the most successful template for the management of pluralism, because, as he states bluntly, "no one has the faintest idea how to do any better."

And what is this magic formula: "By generating the presumption of fair treatment in all public institutions (sometimes through exaggerated, bend-over-backwards gestures of accommodation), the multiculturalism policy encouraged immigrants to venture out of their communities, and join political parties, become police officers, and get jobs in places where everyone speaks the language of the majority."

The recipe is simple: we have to pretend to give fair treatment by exaggerated bend-over-backwards gestures and, by magic, utopia will come forth.

---

[45] This is an op-ed piece by Gilles Paquet sent to the *Ottawa Citizen* on June 19, 2013, that the newspaper refused to publish.

[46] Joseph Heath. 2004. *The Myth of Shared Values in Canada*. Ottawa, ON: Canadian Centre for Management Development.

[47] Joseph Heath. 2013. "How to avoid the next turban controversy," *The Ottawa Citizen*, June 18, A13.

There are many problems with this celebration of deception as national strategy.

One problem is that the success of this strategy is grossly exaggerated. Recent Environics survey results for 2012 suggest that 70 percent of Canadians think that too many immigrants do not adopt Canadian mores – a percentage that has been going up over the last decade.

A second problem is that such a strategy of cultural surrender (real or pretended) is unacceptable to Canadians. This is what Bouchard-Taylor proposed to Quebeckers, and this strategy was massively rejected by the Quebec population. This is why the report was merrily shelved. So suggesting that it be retrieved as a new North Star for Quebec is a non-starter. I suspect that such a strategy of cultural surrender would also be massively rejected by the Canadian population at large, if the question was ever put to them.

The only group seduced by such a strategy would appear to be a certain segment of the Canadian intelligentsia permeated by the politics of guilt: repenting on behalf of their society for past imaginary sins, and willing to impose expiation on the citizenry for such sins by exaggerated bend-over-backwards gestures.[48] In the case of English Canada, the propensity for the intelligentsia to invent past sins (our systematic racism, for instance, according to Stephen Lewis) helps explain the call for expiation and atonement.

A third problem has to do with the ethics of deception as a national strategy. Heath suggests that we only have to pretend to engage in cultural surrender. But pretending is lying, and such pretending is not only intellectually dishonest but also practically very dangerous. For instead of clearly stating that there are some aspects of our common public culture that are non-negotiable, and that those unwilling to accept them should not join our society, we are urged to indulge in institutional lying in the way initiated by former Liberal Minister Sheila Finestone in 1995, when she declared that Canada had no national culture of its own, and that therefore newcomers could bring in their own culture when they move to Canada.

---

[48] Paul Edward Gottfried. 2002. *Multiculturalism and the Politics of Guilt.* Columbia, MO: The University of Missouri Press.

Canada has a common public culture – a set of norms of vivre-ensemble that it has evolved over time and that constitutes the foundation of our way or life. Newcomers have to accept this common public culture. It may evolve over time, but the laws of hospitality require that the newcomers accept them as a condition of entry. Equality of men and women, rule of law, etc. are not negotiable. Not stating it clearly as a condition of entry, and pretending to bend-over-backwards as a strategy of appeasement is a form of deceit. If later we wish to rescind on those exaggerated bend-over-backwards moves, can we be surprised if the newcomers accuse us of having lied and of having acted in bad faith.

A final and more fundamental problem with Joseph Heath's argument is that it is entirely based on a faulty assumption that has been an act of faith of members of the Canadian intelligentsia for decades. Indeed, they have propagandized in a most dishonest way the so-called multicultural assumption that suggests that by such hyper-tolerance and surrender to newcomers' unreasonable requests by the host society, newcomers' integration will automatically follow. This assumption invented by John Berry in the 1970s has been sanctified as gospel truth by multiculturalists. Even though it has been disproven around the world, some Canadian academics remain unshaken in their faith: Canada is an exception, and, in any case, true or not, there is a Canadian consensus about the validity of this assumption! Those refusing to support this act of faith have been accused of bigotry, racism and worse.

So Heath proposes cultural surrender (or at least pretending to do so) as the golden rule. He denounces Quebec's cultural lag in embracing the multicultural faith, and urges Quebeckers to convert to the faith now, for there is no other way. Rarely has the multiculturalist propaganda taken such an overtly self-righteous tone.

A particularly fascinating aspect of this bizarre paper by Joseph Heath is the sort of contorted reasoning he resorts to in order to support his spurious argument. For instance, the aggressive Quebec laïcité policy that would seem to stand in the way of Quebec's cultural surrender is, according to Heath, the result of Quebeckers, having failed to keep their own religion, being led to ordain that others should not be allowed to keep theirs. As for Heath's proposal for righting

Quebec's wrongs, he suggests that the only thing missing on the way to the multiculturalist apotheosis in Quebec is the discovery of a gimmick to ensure that Quebeckers join in the multiculturalist faith without losing face! One more subterfuge! Welcome to the marvelous world of Joseph Heath.

| Sustainability

"But since knowing is what they do, knowledge
is what they look for, and they are likely to give the
name of knowledge to anything they find."

Michael Wood

Introduction

n a world of common-pool resources, or where commons
abound, externalities also abound, the traditional
appropriation systems fail, and the governance challenges
are daunting. Indeed, a whole literature has developed around
the theme of "the tragedy of the commons:" it has shown
that individual rational behaviour is likely, in unregulated
circumstances, to lead to the destruction of the resource. Both
markets and state coercion have revealed their limitations in
coping with such threats.

That is why the governance of sustainability – concerned
with keeping an eye on the changing relations between people
and their socio-physical environment, between the regions
and the contextual ecological systems constituting their life-
support systems – has become such a crucial issue. But debates
about the governance of sustainability have been less than
fruitful because of some *idées fixes*.

First, even though there has been no meaningful support
for radical minority groups' crusades to leave the natural

world unchanged, *environment fetishism* (as Amartya Sen calls it) has not been completely exorcized, either. There is often confusion between sustaining the lives that people can live in an environment, and sustaining the environment itself.

Second, there has been considerable fixation on property rights as a panacea. Whatever the merits of both a sound property rights system and the price mechanism, they do not constitute sufficient conditions for sustainability nor a wise stewardship of nature.

Third, sustainability, *à la* Brundtland-Solow (BS), has become the popular governing relation: taking all the steps necessary to allow the next generation to achieve a standard of living at least as good as our own and to look after the subsequent generation.

Given the fact that even the 2007 report of the Intergovernmental Panel on Climate Change – a strident and alarmist group – suggests that living standards in the developing world a hundred years from now are projected to be some 8.5 times higher than they are today (instead of some 9.5 times higher, without the alleged ravages of climate change)[1] – the Brundtland-Solow standard may not provide much of a guidepost and can be contested.[2] Sustainability is, indeed, an essentially contested concept. It connotes a nexus of issues of such complexity that reasonable and competent persons may hold opposed and contradictory views.

The problems sustainability poses are empirical (socio-economic and political), but additionally, epistemic and moral. Sustainability refers to the empirical ways in which humankind should exploit the resources of nature (and culture) so as to ensure that subsequent generations are not left unduly impoverished. But it also refers to the knowledge system that underpins the goodness of fit between system and

---

[1] Nigel Lawson. 2008. *An Appeal to Reason – Global Warming*. London, UK: Duckworth, p. 93.

[2] Robert M. Solow. 1992. *An Almost Practical Step Toward Sustainability*. Washington, DC: Resources for the Future; Amartya Sen. 2003. "The End and Means of Sustainability" in *Transition to Sustainability in the 21ˢᵗ Century*. Washington, DC: The National Academies Press, p. 2-16.

context, and provides the requisite guideposts for effective and sustainable co-evolution. Finally, it refers to a problem of ethics – a call for inter-generational concerns: the need to give appropriate weight to the concerns of future generations, and the imperatives of wise stewardship in our decision making.

The chapter proceeds in four steps.

First, I ask the basic question, "what should we try to sustain?" and attempt to identify some of the obstacles that prevent social scientists from answering the question satisfactorily. These obstacles are not only the complexity of the issues, but some unfortunate traits of the conventional social sciences: myopia, amnesia, imprudence, etc. Second, I sketch some of the key components of an adequate ecology of governance, based on the principle of subsidiarity, and on loose partnerships, in a context at least partially made of commons. Third, I attempt to identify the sort of *outillage mental* capable of blending the empirical, epistemic and moral challenges of sustainability into a workable governance regime, recognizing that governance can only provide auxiliary conditions for effective co-evolution, and that one must question the unreasonable expectations that have emerged from those quarters that have elected to transmogrify sustainability into some sort of civil theology. Fourth, I make the case for polycentric governance as the most promising strategy, and put forward a few modest general propositions for the families of mechanisms likely to be necessary for effective governance to prevail and hint at what patience and social learning might counsel.

Sustainability as a weaselword

Despite the considerable work focusing on both diagnosing governance failures and on designing institutions for governing the commons better, we are still without a unified theory of sustainable environmental governance. The work on small-scale systems (at the micro level) and on environmental regimes (at the macro level) is interesting, but it has not yet converged on a broadly similar set of questions, activities or governance mechanisms. Indeed, there is still very poor reconciliation between the bottom-up approaches that have been shown to work well, and the aggregative approaches and top-down coercive strategies that continue to mesmerize the technocrats.

The main reason such a unified theory still eludes us is ascribable to two major obstacles.

First, it is due to the essentially contested nature of the notion of sustainability. Second, the road to a general theory is made all the more difficult by the fundamental limitations of traditional social sciences in dealing with such long-run issues.

These two obstacles, when compounded, have tended to derail the debate on sustainability and to facilitate its hijacking by different tribes of ideologues: the *absolutist radicals,* building on moral imperatives and ecological theology; the *politically correct,* who have suppressed most of the important contentious issues and drowned sustainability discussions in banalities; and the *crafty spin doctors,* who have succeeded in using the label as a way to orchestrate public relations cover-ups in the guise of green bottom lines. But some core meaning – a 'vision', in the Schumpeterian sense of the word – has evolved around which an emerging consensus might materialize.

Sustainability as an essentially contested concept

Sustainability has come to connote a whole range of meanings: from the capacity of socio-technical systems to endure and continue indefinitely at one end of the spectrum, to the maintenance of human freedoms at the other.

While environmental fetishism is unduly static, many other less extreme views are equally difficult to defend. For instance, the Brundtland-Solow focus on maintaining the standard of living and consumption that we have grown accustomed to as a norm to be sustained, or the corporate definition of sustainability as "what is corporately viable with minimal impairment to the financial bottom line," are definitions too constrained by strictly economistic considerations.

At the opposite end of the spectrum, Amartya Sen has emphasized the centrality of "sustaining freedoms" as the key objective: maintaining and enhancing the enjoyment of undiminished freedoms (political, social, economic, security, etc.) and avoiding the burden of additional unfreedoms (for development is the removal of various types of unfreedoms).[3] Between those two poles, there are a large number of diverse definitions that have extended the notion of 'sustainability' (originally related mainly to the physical environment) to deal with the much broader notion of 'environment', pertaining not only to the physiographic context, but also to the whole socio-cultural domain. Indeed, it has become less and less clear in 'corporate sustainability reporting', for instance, what is to be 'sustained'. Is it profitability? Is it the corporation? Is it development? Is it the social order? Or is it something else?

Indeed, the shorthand "sustainability reporting" is now used (in the sustainability toolkit of Industry Canada, http://www.sustainabilityreporting.ca) to refer to the broad issue of "how societal trends are affecting the company, and how the company's presence and operations are affecting society." This entails taking into account dozens of reference points ranging all over the economic, financial, environmental and social performance areas of the company.

Depending on the way in which sustainability is defined, there is obviously a great deal of difference in the array of means that can be suggested to achieve the stated goal. The more one leans toward the preservation of nature *qua* nature, the more coercive measures would appear to be required to modify behaviour in order to protect it. The more one leans toward the 'social and cultural' side of sustaining the freedoms alternative, the more one is led to an anthropocentric focus, and to considering behavioural changes through dialogue, deliberation and education.

These various definitions are in use because sustainability is an *essentially contested concept*, the proper use of which inevitably involves endless disputes. According to Gallie, an essentially contested concept is:

---

[3] Amartya Sen. 1999. *Development as Freedom*. New York, NY: Knopf, p. xii.

1) appraisive in the sense that it accredits some kind of valued achievement;
2) this achievement must be complex in character, and its worth attributed to it as a whole; but
3) variously describable in its parts with the possibility of various components being assigned more or less importance;
4) open in character to the extent that it admits considerable modification in the light of changing circumstances; moreover, to qualify as an essentially contested concept; and
5) each party must recognize that its own use of the concept is contested by other parties, and that the concept may be used both aggressively and defensively.[4]

Sustainability is an elusive notion, very much like the notion of championship performance in figure skating.

Governing to steer the system in the direction of such a moving, incommensurable and differently-defined target is, therefore, a task condemned to be difficult.

Limitations of traditional social sciences

But this elusiveness is also ascribable to a large extent to the limitations of traditional social sciences, especially on matters pertaining to the long run.

This fundamental flaw is rooted in the unfortunate influence of positivism on the social sciences, which has resulted in the fixation of the conventional social sciences on prediction and prescription, and to a relative neglect of adequate description.[5] Indeed, even when social scientists indulge in description, it suffers greatly from a focus on *hic et nunc*, and on the bizarre presumption of a world of complete continuity and divisibility.

On the one hand, the propensity to indulge in reductive description leads to the heavy discounting of anything that is not in the present, or in spatial proximity, and therefore to dwarfing the value of any benefit or malefit occurring beyond the now

---

[4] Walter B. Gallie. 1964. *Philosophy and the Historical Understanding.* London, UK: Chatto & Windus, p. 161.
[5] Amartya Sen. 1999. "Galbraith and the Art of Description" in H. Sassoon (ed.). *Between Friends.* New York, NY: Houghton-Mifflin.

or the fringe. Such reductive myopia considerably biases all calculations against taking into account the long run malefits that may be incurred in the remote environment. On the other hand, the assumption of complete divisibility and continuity tends to occlude the possibility of avalanches, irreversibility or discontinuity. These are presumed to be unlikely. *Natura not fecit saltum* is taken as an axiom, and obliterates from the usual calculation the potential for catastrophic events that may cause irreversible damage.

The conventional wisdom *problematique* emphasizes given preferences, static efficiency, and individual rational choice. Such a perspective not only heavily discounts elements that are (1) distant in time and (2) not proximate in space, and pays little attention to (3) learning and dynamic efficiency, or (4) matters of interaction or coordination. Moreover, (5), it relies unduly on a notion of mechanical reversible time that builds myopia, amnesia and imprudence into the conventional practice of these social sciences, and leads them to pay little attention to discontinuities.[6]

These five blind spots have led the traditional social sciences to privilege a sort of cartography of reality lacking in both comprehensiveness and *prudentia*.

It has trapped social scientists into being type I cartographers. As Schumacher has explained, there are two types of cartographers.[7] Type I live by the rule "if in doubt, leave it out," while type II live by the rule "if in doubt, show it prominently." Traditional social sciences have celebrated type I cartographers even though, in our turbulent and

[6] William C. Clark and R.E. Munn (eds.). 1986. *Sustainable Development of the Biosphere.* Cambridge, UK: Cambridge University Press; Michael Redclift. 1987. *Sustainable Development: Exploring the Contradictions.* London, UK: Methuen; David Braybrooke and Gilles Paquet. 1987. "Human Dimensions of Global Change: The Challenges to the Humanities and Social Sciences," *Transactions of the Royal Society of Canada*, Fourth Series, vol. XXV, p. 269-291; Paul Laurent and Gilles Paquet. 1998. *Epistémologie et économie de la relation : coordination et gouvernance distribuée.* Paris/Lyon, FR: Vrin, chapter 4; Raymond Boudon. 2003. *Raison, bonnes raisons.* Paris, FR: Presses Universitaires de France.
[7] E.F. Schumacher. 1977. *A Guide for the Perplexed.* New York, NY: Harper & Row.

totally connected world, we may actually need more type II cartographers – for the unsuspected major falls might be just around the next river bend.

Sustainability as sustaining whatever anyone wishes to sustain

The combination of an essentially contested concept, and of the handicaps of conventional social sciences, has led to the promotion of the most whimsical notions of sustainability. Sustainability has become synonymous with sustaining whatever anyone wishes to sustain, for whatever reason. But despite these difficulties, a 'vision' of sustainability has begun to emerge, built around a number of core beliefs that have begun to generate a minimal consensus: a sense of limits, of irreversibility, of co-evolution, a need to sustain our inheritance and our degrees of freedom, etc.[8]

This vision does not provide a conceptual framework capable of generating theoretical propositions, but it would appear to suggest approaches that are pluralistic, i.e., that are using multiple different frameworks.[9] What it demands is "appreciation" à la Vickers,[10] i.e., making judgments of facts and value about the state of the system both internally and in its external relations. These entail the readiness to see and value the situation from a plurality of viewpoints. Indeed, the dream or fantasy of "unity" and "coherence" is a major source of the difficulty, for it stands in the way of the search for effective responses.

This form of loose appreciative framework (to the extent that it embeds mutual inconsistencies) generates considerable frustration from those who wish to predict and prescribe. This explains the popularity of the "escapist" simplistic images in good currency in the face of a complex issue domain, marred by essentially contested concepts and crippling epistemology,

---

[8] Richard B. Norgaard. 1999. *Vision and Methods of Ecological Economics*. Buenos Aires, Argentina: Universidad de Buenos Aires, 16p.

[9] François Perroux. 1960. *Economie et société*. Paris, FR: Presses Universitaires de France.

[10] Goeffrey Vickers. 1965. *The Art of Judgment*. London, UK: Methuen.

ideology as a form of false consciousness thrives, and everyone feels empowered and legitimized in imposing his/her own partial notion of sustainability as dictated by his/her own interests.

The "market," "business" and "deep ecology" approaches are examples of selective attention being given to one dimension of the problem. In their search for comfort, they privilege either an act of faith in property rights-cum-market mechanisms as panaceas, or a broadening of perspective (to include such an array of social and environmental dimensions that one can easily fuzzify the whole picture), or a fixation on geo-centric, bio-centric or theo-centric oracles.[11]

The same may be said about the environmental rights-based approach: there is a sharpness to rights (easily transformed into entitlements, powers, or immunities) that does not match the fuzziness and complexities of the environmental world. Insisting on legislating what one might best see as ethical claims can only lead to using instruments that will prove unduly intrusive and mostly ineffective.

The freedom-based pluralistic approach suggested by Sen focuses on the truly important dimensions of sustainability, i.e., the degrees of freedom to be preserved for the next generations (economic and financial, but also political and social) and concerns for transparency, security, legitimacy and participation. But it remains rather vague. Since humans are explicitly placed in a context that requires attention to the natural world, Sen's approach need not deny some taking into account of environmental dimensions,[12] but it does not answer the key questions: what should we try to sustain to ensure sustaining freedoms, and how can this be done?

---

[11] Charles Perrings. 1987. *Economy and Environment*. Cambridge, UK: Cambridge University Press; Stratos Inc. 2003. *Building Confidence: Corporate Sustainability Reporting in Canada*. Ottawa, ON; James E. Lovelock. 1979. *GAIA: A New Look at Life on Earth*. Oxford, UK: Oxford University Press; Bill Devall and George Sessions. 1985. *Deep Ecology: Living as if Nature Mattered*. Layton, UT: Gibbs M. Smith Inc.; Herman E. Daly and John B. Cobb jr. 1989. *For the Common Good*. New York, NY: Beacon Press.

[12] Hugh P. McDonald. 2004. *John Dewey and Environmental Philosophy*. Albany, NY: State University of New York Press.

Governance

Government cannot just respond to the sustainability challenge by fiat or decrees. What needs to be sustained does not necessarily fall under the control of governments who are not in possession of all the required information, power or resources to get other agents to modify their behaviour in any particular direction. A workable strategy must mobilize the public, private and civic sectors, and build on their collaboration.

Governments must change their role: they must cease to be controllers, and become catalysts and *animateurs*. This is the drift from government to governance that has been extensively analyzed.[13]

Mixed organizations

There has been a significant growth of mixed organizations to deal with the challenges at hand, because they combine the features of the three basic mechanisms at work in the three sectors: coercion, *quid pro quo* exchange and reciprocity in the long-term horizon; and fair stewardship of the public sector; the creativity and dynamism of the private sector; and the compassion, commitment and trust in the not-for-profit sector.

These "partnerships" have proven effective. What may at first have been mainly opportunistic efforts to take advantage of certain specific skills of sub-contractors (with the need to constrain them with strong legal contracts and numerous specific requirements and penalty clauses) has often evolved into true joint venturing based on a flexible, continuing relationship, rooted in loose arrangements to respond to the evolving expectations and needs of the other parties, and in soft horizontal accountabilities. The parties must be mutually accountable. Such accountabilities must provide the sorts of incentives needed for the parties both to wish to join the game in the first place, and to ensure that they will meet their commitments even if and when it might not be to their short-term advantage to do so. As the strength of the partnerships

---

[13] Gilles Paquet. 1999. "Innovations in Governance in Canada," *Optimum, The Journal of Public Sector Management*, 29(2-3): 71-81.

grows, the underlying conventions require less and less formality. But this generates an immense problem when it comes to the definition of performance or the fair sharing of the surplus.

Because of these challenges, partnerships at first glance may appear to be unmanageable. In fact, in a concrete setting, committed partners find ways to co-design viable arrangements, even when each of them has a different frame of reference. Indeed, it is as a result of this very process of co-design that the intentions and meanings of each partner are revealed, and that negotiation in a situated context can be conducted. Such a process of co-design helps (1) to identify the sorts of interfaces likely to exist, and on which one might build partnerships; but also (2) where compromises might be sought; and (3) ways in which the 'proceeds' may be shared. Since the partners may not all be after the same sort of loot, sharing the proceeds in specific circumstances may not be as intractable a problem as might be anticipated.

This is not the place for an inventory of all the possible rationales partners may harbour as they first enter into a collaborative arrangement. But it is important to underline a few ideas that have been widely noted in the specialized literature. First, partnership may simply be a device to trigger management reform, using partnerships as a way to destabilize the system. The partner is an *agent of subversion*. Second, the objective may also be to effect a problem conversion – a way to redefine the business one is in through some reframing. The partner is an *agent of seduction* that helps elicit a different way of tackling a task: for example, brokering a public interest issue, like environment protection, into one that is of interest to entrepreneurs. Third, partnership may be sought for the purpose of moral regeneration: to inject a concern for the long run in myopic quarterly-earnings-fixated organizations. The partner is an *agent of moral refurbishment*. Fourth, partnership is also an instrument of risk shifting. It is a way of unloading onto the partner a portion of the responsibility for some commitment. The partner becomes an *agent of risk sharing*. Fifth, partnership may simply be a mode of power-sharing, for it is recognized that no one party has the resources, information and power to govern appropriately. The partner is an *agent of cooperation*.[14]

Most partnerships are based on a mix of these rationales: they are multi-purposed instruments used for various reasons. Indeed, most of the time, partnerships are not clearly defined *ab ovo*. They emerge from cautious and limited arrangements into deeper and more robust partnerships through unpredictable meanderings. This has been the experience in the Gulf of Maine, and with the World Weather Watch, where limited information-sharing has led to robust forms of collaborative governance.[15]

If partnerships fail, it is usually because, along the way, the partners refuse to accept the basic conditions of power sharing. One partner or another wants to use partnership as a tool to reform, convert, rekindle or shift risk, but without paying the price of relinquishing some power, accepting the need to negotiate fair terms of agreement, developing relational capital and trust, etc. The result is a bogus partnership, bound to fail. Fortunately, partners who know that they are in the game for the long run appear to be willing to pay the price.

Collaboration and social learning

The core contribution of these partnerships is to the construction of collective intelligence and to the fostering of social learning. Social learning is the interactive process by which individuals and organizations learn from each other, adapt, innovate and, consequently develop new arrangements and conventions among themselves, leading to new rules of behaviour. It is through social learning and its resultant increase in collective intelligence that a community may harness its intellectual, informational, physical and human resources to produce a continuous flow of innovative and

---

[14] Pauline Vaillancourt Rosenau. 2000. *Public Private Policy Partnerships*. Cambridge, MA: The MIT Press.

[15] P.C. Schroeder, P.R. Boudreau, C.E.W. Brehme, A.M. Boyce, A.J. Evans and A. Rahmani. 2001. "The Gulf of Maine Environmental Information Exchange: Participation, Observations, Conversation," *Environment and Planning B: Planning and Design*, 28(6): 865-887; Harlan Cleveland. 2002. "Innovative Technology: The Institutional Challenge," *Chaordic Commons*, 2(1).

usable knowledge. Collective intelligence refers to the creative and discriminative capacities of a community, and effective social learning increases collective intelligence over time. Collective learning requires a context that allows for meaningful conversations to be conducted, and these conversations, deliberations and accumulation of judgments require a capacity to support and to integrate the multiple logics of community members in an atmosphere of tact and civility. This sort of learning does not necessarily result in formalized decision making and conclusions. It often remains as tacit knowledge – a fuzzy implicit recognition of the local and particular context. This is where the communities of practice have the most impact.

This sort of collaborative dynamic requires technologies and mechanisms of collaboration. But such technologies and mechanisms must fit the context. One of the most important challenges is to design governance mechanisms in keeping with the complexity and deep interdependence of the environmental context. Many have emphasized the complexity of the environment because it is an open-system and is effected by the non-linear impacts of any policy intervention. This has led Audrey Doerr to suggest that a Vickersian approach would appear very well suited to the challenges at hand.[16]

In Vickers's world, governing is not built on goals and objectives, or even on setting permanent governing relations. It is an on-going process that involves the evolution and modification of the standards and norms within a context where interdependencies impose constraints and place limits on what the very possibilities of an organization are.[17] Governing requires setting up the largest number of quick feedback learning loops. It seeks behaviour modification through persuasion, participation and perseverance.

[16] Audrey Doerr. 2003. "Perspectives on Policy and Science: Building Bridges for Sustainable Development," (mimeo, 23p).
[17] Geoffrey Vickers. 1968. *Value Systems and Social Process*. London, UK: Tavistock Publications; Geoffrey Vickers. 1983. *Human Systems are Different*. London, UK: Harper & Row.

These mechanisms may take many forms: roundtables, forums, networks, coordination agreements, etc. They must focus on communications as a way to improve the broader arrangement of governing relationships, and the adoption and adaptation of new norms. Such mechanisms have to get away from the seduction of ethereal long-term trends and focus on generating multilogues that are inclusive, integrated and relevant for the ordinary citizen. This is the only way to generate a change in the appreciative system and, therefore, to modify behaviour.

Ecology of governance

One of the most important lessons that would appear to be most difficult to learn is the realization that the law of requisite variety calls for an ecology of governance to regulate the world of sustainability, and that an ecology of governance is anything but integrated and neat.

W.T. Anderson has made the points vividly:

Complex systems cannot be governed effectively from a single center... What we have and are likely to have for some time is what I call an ecology of governance: many different systems and different kinds of systems interacting with one another, like the multiple organisms in an ecosystem. This won't necessarily be neat, peaceful, stable or efficient; despite what some nature lovers may believe, ecosystems are not necessarily neat, peaceful, stable or efficient either ... it will be in a continual process of learning and changing and responding to feedback.[18]

An ecology of governance entails a variety of things: (1) a 'thick' understanding of environmental decision making; (2) a new way of thinking about social-ecological resilience; (3) a mix of co-evolving institutions, processes and ideas from the private, public and social sectors, leading to a form of 'regulated' self-regulation; and (4) effective transition management.

---

[18] Walter T. Anderson. 2001. *All Connected Now.* Boulder, CO: Westview Press, p. 251-252.

Only a 'thick description' – identifying the basic connections and general patterns that are characteristic of a certain context – is likely to lead to decisions that are legitimate and context-sensitive (efficient, effective and equitable).[19] This, in turn, calls for more emphasis on the institutional framing and embeddedness of decisions. Decisions are taken in various arenas of action that influence the behaviour of actors, but the contexts are all continually evolving, and generate institutional creations that follow different rules of decision making and interact in complex and changing ways. Without a thick description, decisions are likely to be made on the basis of false or incomplete information and are, therefore, wrongheaded.

Intervention must be seen as efforts to "sustain and enhance the capacity of social-ecological systems to cope with, adapt to, and shape change."[20] This puts the notion of resilience (and its flip side, vulnerability) front and centre. The central question is to identify behavioural responses that sustain social-ecological systems – and therefore sustain freedoms – in a world that is constantly changing.

Folke has identified four critical factors to understand the dynamics of resilience: learning to live with change and uncertainty, nurturing diversity for renewal, combining different types of knowledge for learning, and creating opportunity for self-organization. These factors entail a new way of thinking about resilience. It is not only a capacity to spring back undiminished aftershocks, it is the capacity for self-renewal, a self-re-creation that allows an organization to learn its way out of evolving predicaments, through making the highest and best use of all the knowledge (whatever its form) from the different stakeholders. Consequently, the governance of sustainability goes well beyond traditional state-centric,

[19] W. Neil Adger et al. 2002. "Governance for Sustainability: Towards a 'Thick' Understanding of Environmental Decision Making." CSERGE Working Paper EDM 02-04, University of East Anglia, UK.
[20] Carl Folke. 2003. "Social-Ecological Resilience and Behavioural Responses" in A. Biel et al. (eds.). *Individual and Structural Determinants of Environmental Practice*. London, UK: Ashgate.

top-down policy making. It is a mix of ideas (awareness, knowledge, approaches, rules), processes (mechanisms and linkages) and institutions (roundtables, research units) rooted in all sectors, and it needs to be somewhat coordinated.

Some have argued that the decentralized Canadian model of governance of sustainability has significant limitations because of its fragmentation. They have called for a fuller and more coercive role for central agencies. This is ill-inspired. While the decentralized model is imperfect, it is the most promising strategy. Governance clearly takes place in multiple arenas, partly within and partly outside the scope of the state. It involves polycentric steering institutions, with a strong emphasis on subsidiarity, which has become a prominent guiding principle. This co-evolutionary, polycentric governance approach calls for a mix of institutions, puts emphasis on knowledge generation, and uses targets not as absolute objectives, but as a set of incentives to readjust expectations, change habits, and search for a new direction of innovation.[21]

Transition management is necessary because of two important sets of obstacles or barriers to the emergence of a coherent ecology of governance: (1) the fact that the governance schemes are often locked into short-term benefits trajectories; and (2) the fact that there is much fragmentation in the issue domain, leaving the various policy fields somewhat disconnected at times. In that context, transition management is soft planning and an exercise in *vision-led incrementalism*: it feeds adaptive, interactive, and multilevel governance, and improves them through taking into account long-term sustainability visions. Transitions are not blueprints: they are long-term-oriented evolutionary processes that do no more than create possible development pathways, arenas capable of generating evolving agendas and experiments.[22]

[21] Raimund Bleischwitz and Thomas Langrock. 2003. "Governance of Sustainable Development – Coevolution of Corporate and Political Strategies," (mimeo).

[22] This may be done either directly, or through the development of monitoring and evaluation mechanisms underpinning short learning loops. David Loorbach. 2007. *Transition Management – New Modes of Governance for Sustainable Development*. Rotterdam, Netherlands: International Books.

Blending, complex adaptive systems and *bricolage*

The governance of sustainability consists of maintaining through time a complex pattern of relationships within limits that have somehow come to be set as governing relations. Such governing relations define a corridor, evolving through time and aiming at making possible a regime more acceptable to all concerned than the logic of the situation would otherwise provide. This runs contrary to the conventional taste for comprehensive and centralized planning – considered as the only way to avoid chaos.

Such governing relations are built on a blending of many perspectives, an appreciation of the dynamics of complex adaptive systems and a recognition that thoughtful interventions often cannot be more than *bricolage*.

Blending

Blending is a generative cognitive operation (on a par with analogy, mental modeling, framing) that produces a conceptual structure not provided by the perspectives that serve as inputs. It generates new viewpoints partly on the basis of old.[23] It serves a variety of cognitive purposes: triggering ideas, arguments and inferences developed in the blend that have effects on cognition. Blending also contributes to consensus building.

There are three operations in the construction of the blend: composition, completion and elaboration. These three operations lead to the emergent perspective or mental space of the blend. Composition provides the new frame and relations that did not exist in the input spaces; completion draws from the background knowledge to complete the pattern; elaboration develops the blend through imaginative mental exploration.

In the case of sustainability, there may be a wide variety of blends that could be instrumental in forging new consensuses in a variety of contexts. For the purpose of general illustration, one might use the blend of the three perspectives referred to

[23] Mark Turner. 2001. *Cognitive Dimensions of Social Science*. Oxford, UK: Oxford University Press.

earlier: sustainability as an empirical/institutional challenge, as an epistemic challenge, and as an ethical challenge. If successful, such blending provides an emergent meaning that underpins governing relations.

The first perspective is focused on institutional design and the self-reinforcing mechanisms that generate behavioural learning, i.e., learning that builds on past experience to respond to new situations. But existing institutions and their collective memory suffer from *structural amnesia.*[24] The institutions doing the recognizing and the classifying of the risks worth taking into account may systematically disregard problems that would threaten values and deconstruct institutions. Even when the basic facts are confirmed, there is no assurance that they will become socially defined as problems worth worrying about.

The second perspective is focused on *usable ignorance,* i.e., on an awareness of our own ignorance, and on learning designed with the ignorance factor in mind. Such learning occurs through environmental representations that are reframed and strategies consequently being modified. This evolution is always unfinished: a culture is always imperfectly adjusted, because actors have imperfect and incomplete information and limited rationality, and because adjustments take time.

The third perspective is based on *trans-science,* i.e., on questions that cannot be answered by science, that 'transcend' science. Sustainability is a subject matter too complex and too variable for only scientific canons to apply; moral judgments are involved.[25]

Blending composes the elements (institutional, epistemic, moral) of the input spaces into a new space that recognizes the multidimensionality of sustainability, and attempts to merge them into a pattern of learning: learning from the past, learning from usable ignorance, and learning from appreciation and judgment, rather than only from so-called facts. Such blends are at the core of social learning. They play the same role as prototypes in learning, in general. A child learns the notion of

[24] Clark and Munn, 1986, *op.cit.*, p. 433.
[25] Alvin M. Weinberg. 1974. "Science and Trans-Science," *Minerva*, 10(2): 209-222.

a bird through a prototype – a sparrow – and the rest of his life will be simply the story of how he/she adds some flats and sharps to this prototype to encompass penguins and ostriches.[26] The most interesting aspect of blending is obviously elaboration – the imaginative extension of whatever space has ensued to generate a dynamic blend with a life of its own, capable of carrying the argument further.

The blend that is mapping the *problematique* of the governance of sustainability (a composite vision or provisional arrangement of the objects of the inquiry into a pattern) remains quite blurred. But its construction is the major challenge facing environmentalists. Without it, one does not have the required complex image of the system to be governed or the basic pluralistic *outillage mental* needed not only to grapple with this complex system but also to elaborate an evolving guiding vision and elicit a workable regime.

Complex adaptive system

A provisional blend that can serve in guiding the learning process about sustainability is the notion of a complex adaptive system. It is a notion that encompasses the institutional, the epistemic, and the moral dimensions that are of interest.

A complex adaptive system (CAS) is first and foremost a system, i.e., it is composed of a structure (a set of roles and relationships among actors), a technology (the tools and techniques that extend the human capability of its members), and a theory (views held within the system about its purposes, its operations, and its future). These dimensions are interdependent, so that any change in one produces change in the others.[27]

This interacting and evolving set of individuals and groups, bound together by structures, technologies, and theory, has certain features: (1) it is *open,* and receives resources from the external environment; (2) it must *adapt* to its environment through modifications of its social and

[26] Mark Johnson. 1993. *Moral Imagination.* Chicago, IL: The University of Chicago Press.

[27] Donald A. Schön. 1971. *Beyond The Stable State.* New York, NY: Norton, p. 33-36.

technical texture; (3) this entails a process of *differentiation* to respond to the different challenges posed by the environment; (4) this generates a system of *interactions* so complex that agents cannot analyze them *ex ante;* they must simply *adapt and discover* new rules and new behaviours that generate the requisite *coordination and integration* for the system's high performance to ensue – as they proceed.

Any CAS (like our central nervous system, our immune system or our ecosystem) is made up of parts that are well interconnected, where complexity and organization arise non-linearly from interaction. The system is self-organizing, and is guided by vague schemata or templates that evolve through Darwinian selection and guide the system to disattend to aspects of experience. Such a CAS develops a variety of schemata, often highly local and provisional, as recognition devices, and their evolution is path-dependent, contingent and based upon developed, entrenched patterns.

While such a blend is intellectually satisfying, it resembles early maps – elegant but not necessarily very helpful to navigation. Much refinement is therefore required if the sort of governance relations required are to be diagnosed pragmatically, and to design them accordingly, and allow them to develop creatively. But work in progress is already showing the way. Indeed, for the last 10 years, James Kay (and his colleagues and graduate students) has been using an ecosystem approach to sustainability, and has gained considerable recognition for the sort of governance arrangements that are suggested for complex settings.[28]

Kay's work suggests that the best we can hope for is to create conditions that may lead to the requisite cooperation for effective governance. New rules and new behaviours have to be discovered along the way. This provides a sharply deflated vision of what can be accomplished through governing.

Taking advantage of these organic and emergent forces means living with complexity and harnessing it. This

---

[28] James Kay et al. 1999. "An Ecosystem Approach to Sustainability: Addressing the Challenge of Complexity," *Futures*, 31(7): 721-742.

perspective is predicated on an acknowledgment of our ignorance. It is the reason massive mechanical interventions often prove futile, while relatively small interventions, that make the highest and best use of the inner dynamics of the system, may be surprisingly effective. These paradoxical results are ascribable to the lesser or better way of taking into account the reactions of mutually adaptive players to interventions that promote (or not) effective adaptation, fruitful interactions and powerful social learning. Since not enough is known to control the system, the best that can be done is to experimentally provoke some variation, interaction and selection processes by thoughtful interventions.[29]

Bricolage

These small thoughtful interventions may attempt to modify the actors' time horizon, to accelerate the process of social learning, to tinker with interaction patterns by modifying proximity and space, or by creating shared space or forums, by sharpening performance measurements, and helping to catalyze a better selection of agents and strategies. But in all these interventions, it must be understood that what can be expected at best is to stimulate and 'excite' the complex adaptive system without any guarantee that the desired outcome will be reached.

Reform must accompany the system, rather than try to remake it. Muddling through and *bricolage* are thus more valuable than disruptive and so-called transformative restructuring.

In ascertaining the sort of intervention that might be most helpful in the case of the environment, some guidance may be derived from an examination of interventions in the health care system, as an example of a complex adaptive system in need of repairs.

What has been proposed in the case of the health care system is less a complete revamping of the system than: (1) a multiplication of access and information points; (2) more transparency about waiting time; (3) multiple service lines within emergency rooms; (4) increased support for caregivers

[29] Robert Axelrod and Michael D. Cohen. 1999. *Harnessing Complexity*. New York, NY: The Free Press, p. xv.

and self-caregivers, etc.[30] On the supply side, this has translated into rewards for differentiated knowledge, respect for complementary professional perspectives, no disruption of a workable division of labour, etc.

The challenge is to identify particularly effective tipping points, capable of triggering the equivalent of epidemics, and making full use of the power of context.

A plea for polycentric governance

In the face of such a messy situation (sustainability as sustained freedoms; high level of turbulence and uncertainty; ill-defined and ill-structured problems; likelihood of irreversible discontinuities; wide distribution of resources, power and information; no unified view of environmental governance and the need for ecologies of governance; a complex adaptive system and the need to be satisfied with *bricolage*), it is important to draw some conclusions about the sort of governance of sustainability that is likely to be workable.

One of the important results of the work of the last quarter century on the governance of common-pool resources has been that polycentricity works best. Only this type of governance can nurture the communities' self-governing capabilities.

Polycentricity is a *manière de voir* that is built on two presumptions: (1) that there is no single source of authority vested with all the power, resources, information and legitimacy, which also has the exclusive responsibility for determining public policy; (2) that the diversity of circumstances calls for a diversity of arrangements that may appear overwhelming and even ungovernable at first, and most certainly not very neat, until it is realized that such is the case only from the viewpoint of the centralizing mindset, and that it need not be so once the perspective point is modified and the powers of self-governance are allowed to unfold.

---

[30] Sholom Glouberman and Brenda Zimmerman. 2002. "Complicated and Complex Systems: What Would Successful Reform of Medicare Look Like," Discussion Paper 8 (Ottawa, ON: Romanow Commission on the Future of Health Care in Canada), p. 24.

Self-governance flows naturally from the principle of subsidiarity that suggests that decision making should be located at the most local level where it can be efficiently and effectively executed, and that higher level decision making should prevail only when local and lower level instances have demonstrated that they cannot do it well, or at all. So self-governance does not entail a chaotic or disorderly division of labour among sectors and levels of organizations, but an ecology of loosely coupled arrangements, likely to be most effective in ensuring that adjustment tasks are delegated to the sub-systems that can handle them best. It is a commitment to as much decentralization as possible, and as much centralization as necessary.

The way to get there may not be very clear but a number of modest general propositions can be put forward that might be subsumed under three general rubrics: loosely coupled arenas, learning through multilogue and triggers for social learning.

Loosely coupled arenas
Open systems evolution is dictated to a large extent by external pressures. Yet the vulnerability of open systems to external shocks can be mitigated somewhat, and some stability ensured, through a partitioning of the system into loosely coupled segments. This allows the segments best able to do so to react to certain external shocks, and to provide the adjustments required. Multi-stability is thereby acquired. Multi-stability entails a fragmentation into sub-systems, and a degree of decentralization of decision making toward arenas where the challenges can best be handled. These segments are built around arenas where communities of practice, networks of persons, and groups with some stake in the issues, etc., congregate to shape the *modus vivendi*, or at least to defend their interests.

Most of the time, governing requires a focus on what Les Metcalfe would call the three Ds: *diagnosis*, *design* and *development*.[31] Issue areas therefore generate arenas where

[31] Les Metcalfe. 1993. "Public Management: From imitation to innovation" in Jan Kooiman (ed.). *Modern Governance: New Government-Society Interactions*. London, UK: Sage Publications, p. 173-189.

they can be debated, and where governance responses can be designed.

As society becomes more diverse and volatile, the likelihood of governing failures through disconcertation increases, and it becomes clear that such a dynamic, complex and diverse world can only be governed in a complex, dynamic and diverse way, through modes of governance that will vary according to time, place and circumstances.

While there is an assumption implicit in much of conventional thinking that governments and states may ordain such responses, this is questionable. Citizens and groups more and more refuse to be governed top-down without their consent. Moreover, the degree of complexity, diversity and dynamism in open systems is such that they have become *de facto* ungovernable from the centre. Consequently, one must face the dual challenge of (1) living by the principle of *subsidiarity*; and (2) working at defining the *optimal structuration*, i.e., the optimal partitioning and division of labour among sectors and between levels. This calls for a much higher degree of decentralization than the conventional wisdom would appear to favour.

From this perspective, it is possible to derive a few modest general propositions.

Governance of sustainability aims at behaviour modification, is anchored and develops in multiple arenas, and must be deeply rooted at the local level.

This range of stakeholders is quite different from place to place and time to time. Workable arrangements will not take the same form in all arenas, and the policy instrument choice is likely to differ according to circumstances. The principle of subsidiarity is likely to be the dominant force. This is an imperative that contradicts the states' propensity to centralize, but one that experts in the field have long recognized. What is required is a redesigned institutional order, and loosely coupled domains of governance that would be quite different from one another.

This need not imply incoherence, but only questions the usefulness of homogeneity and standardization in a world that is diverse. Behaviour modification entails learning, and learning is maximized when the agent closest to the context, and confronted with it, is faced with making the adaptation. Indeed, *in situ*, what might appear to be intractable, in theory, gets resolved.[32] As a result, organizations and agents evolve; they become different from what they used to be. This is the essence of learning. And it happens more easily locally.

Governance of sustainability relies on "regulated" self-regulation. Governance in this new context is seen as "regulated self-regulation." It recognizes the multiplicity of loci where decisions are taken, and the need for polycentric steering institutions with as much self-regulation as possible, although it also provides for as much imposed regulation as necessary. Such regulation may take different forms (property rights regime, stabilization, insurance, regulation, conflict management, etc.) but most importantly it must provide fail-safe mechanisms when self-regulation appears to fail.

This obviously means that the regulatory system has to be strengthened in order to deter corporations from acting against the public interest (significant liability for directors and managers, graduated fines for offences, exclusion from public markets in the case of repeated offences, and even "suspending the charters of corporations that flagrantly and persistently violate the public interest,"[33] or seeking a court order to dissolve a corporation, take its assets, and sell it at public auction to those who will operate it in the public interest).

While there have been hesitations (and rightly so) to use the precautionary principle to prescribe legally that "corporations be prohibited from acting in ways that are reasonably likely to cause harm, even if definitive proof that such harm will occur does not exist"[34] (because of the possible abuses to which it might lead), ways must be found to bring forth the spirit of the precautionary principle into the regulatory regime, even if it is not in the law.

[32] Donald A. Schön and Martin Rein. 1994. *Frame Reflection*. New York, NY: Basic Books.

[33] Joel Bakan. 2004. *The Corporation*. Toronto, ON: Viking Canada, p. 161.

[34] *Ibid.*, p. 162.

Learning through multilogue.

The core of the arena is communication. As Yankelovich puts it: "dialogue is a process of successful relationship building."[35]

Vickers has identified five levels of communication: communication by (1) threat, (2) bargaining, (3) request, (4) persuasion, and (5) dialogue.[36] This emphasizes the growth in the minimal trust and understanding necessary for communication to proceed: each level demanding from each party to communicate a more complex and reliable model of the other, or more trust in the other, or both. As Vickers suggests, negotiation may be no more than level 1 or 2, but may also rise to level 5.

The extraordinary experience of General Agreement on Tariffs and Trade (GATT) – what economists have come to call the General Agreement on Talking and Talking – in generating a negotiated agreement to reducing international tariffs from some 45 percent in 1945 to an insignificant level in the year 2000, has been built on a multilogue marred by very little executive power. While it may not have been designed as such, and may even be the successful result of an institution many dominant countries wanted to remain a toothless tiger, GATT has proved to be a most impressive success.

One of the extraordinary weaknesses in our modern governance institutions is the lack of places, sites, or loci for multilogue. This is true at the local, national and international levels. Unless such forums exist where citizens cannot only become conscious of the issues, but can reflect, confront their perspectives, beliefs and opinions, and deliberate, little social learning will ensue.

Such forums must be inclusive and permeate the whole of society if they are to be effective. Closed forums of experts (often with closed minds) are not very effective: they preach to the converted, and generate debates that produce more heat than light, since experts often claim to know it all (or almost

---

[35] Daniel Yankelovich. 1999. *The Magic of Dialogue.* New York, NY: Simon & Schuster, p. 15.

[36] Geoffrey Vickers 1987. *Policy-making, Comunication, and Social Learning.* New Brunswick, NJ: Transaction, chapter 8.

all) to begin with. This is why those roundtable exercises (of a closed and experts-only variety), that it was hoped would be useful in allowing the new forms of governance of sustainability to emerge, have often floundered. They have neither been successful in reaching out to the citizenry nor in driving out corrupt communication. For there is in communication the equivalent of Gresham's Law in economics: bad communication drives out good communication.[37]

From this perspective, one may also derive a few modest general propositions.

Governance of sustainability demands short feedback learning loops.

Communication and deliberation are meant to generate better understanding and greater trust. But another function of communication is watching for signs of misunderstanding and errors, in order to correct them. So it is not sufficient to have public spaces for deliberation. Deliberations have to be able to generate learning. As it stands now, much of the discussion in open forums is marred by a high degree of cognitive dissonance and political correctness. This means that multiple monologues ensue: an undue amount of tact and civility often entails little learning.

One of the most important indirect and subtle techniques to foster social learning has been the development of voluntary reporting procedures. These are often innocuous processes that appear at first to be both unhelpful and likely to generate much disinformation. For instance, there was a great deal of skepticism when corporations were urged to report on their sustainability strategies.

While in many cases this has led to tepid exercises in public relations, based on very little accomplishment, it has also generated a momentum for better reporting tools, more imaginative ways of gauging the impact of activities purportedly geared to improving sustainability, and an educational thrust that has led to the production of various sustainability indexes. These instruments remain

[37] *Ibid.*, p. 125.

rudimentary, but have begun to have an impact on the climate of opinion.

Governance of sustainability requires experimental prototypes with which to play.

In environmental governance, as in other domains, the 'best' is enemy of the 'good'. Being overly ambitious often leads to a quest for comprehensive approaches, and such approaches often stall all potential corrective activities until a comprehensive plan is available (which is often socially costly), or even make the situation worse, when the plan is implemented in a top-down insensitive way.

One of the important impediments to learning is the belief that one can optimize. In fact, in the face of complex issues, one must be ready to experiment with quick-and-dirty prototypes that can serve as a medium for fruitful conversations and a basis for co-development. Otherwise, little can be accomplished.

As Schrage puts it, "creating a dialogue between people and prototypes is more important than creating a dialogue between people alone."[38] Prototypes are, as we have argued earlier, at the core of learning. There must be a prototype to begin with, if flats and sharps are going to play their role.

Therefore, a spirit of experimentation must be developed if one is to foster social learning, and such experimentation requires a great dose of imagination and gumption. Those virtues are not, for the time being, in good currency, any more than those other politically incorrect virtues: compromise and patience.

Triggering social learning

Even though there may be platforms and arenas where multilogues may be carried out, the sustainability file suffers from many major handicaps: the great amount of ignorance about the dynamics of our planet in the long run; the propensity to treat this nexus of trans-scientific problems as one that scientists can rule over; and the quasi-religious zeal and vehement self-righteousness with which eco-fundamentalism

---

[38] Michael Schrage. 2000. *Serious Play*. Boston, MA: Harvard Business School Press, p. 15.

articulates its lobbying and advocacy for a reductive and ideology-laden position. These mental prisons stunt the conversation and social learning.

A number of sensible things can be done to attenuate the toxic effects of these blockages.

First, one must underline the importance of comparative monitoring and the need to maintain an open mind about the great variety of sources of the erosion of sustainability, in the case of global warming, for instance. The fact that so much depends on conjecture on the basis of limited information, requires that extrapolations and catastrophic scenarios generated by opaque and grossly imperfect simulation models be used with immense care. They are, at best, partial exploratory devices, and should be treated as such. Consequently, such extrapolations should not be regarded as providing answers to the questions about sustainability, but only hypotheses about what stylized outcomes might look like. These exercises should not authorize willful blindness to data that do not fit the thesis, and vilification of other reputable experts (grouped under the assassin label of *deniers*), who are contesting the progressive alarmist ideology. The media, which has been playing strictly the role of uncritical echo box for sensationalist hypothesizing, should be regarded as such – and not vindicating the canonical position in any way.[39]

The citizenry should be reminded that this is a trans-scientific issue, and that ignorance is immense. This will ensure that the problem is not mis-specified, and that those grappling with the scientific components of it are not allowed, on the basis of partial knowledge and speculations, to become the opinion moulders.

Second, the quasi-religious zeal of eco-fundamentalism has acquired such a force that it has considerably biased the multilogues around sustainability issues. The only way to counter that influence is to reframe the issue as a matter of behavioural change. It calls for a mix of incentive reward (economic) and moral contract (socio-psychological-ethical),

[39] Nigel Lawson, 2008, *op.cit.*, chapter 8.

insisting that (1) the technological forces that might provide capacity to counter negative forces, (2) the need and capacity by the current population to adapt to new conditions, and (3) the ethical dimensions of putting the full onus of the adjustment on the present generation with little concern for the differential carrying capacities of the present and future cohorts, all be taken into account. Such considerations (factoring in technical change, adaptability and the greater capability of future generations to shoulder the adjustment) obviously lead to much less alarmist conclusions than those built on simulation models.[40]

For the time being, the new religion of eco-fundamentalism, and the Gore-style alarmism generating an unthinking *urgence d'agir* in the face of so much ignorance and uncertainty, are bound to trigger ill-informed, imprudent and impatient policy actions by those who see themselves as the clergy of this new religion.

Rejecting such an approach does not mean inaction.

An experiment with a modest carbon tax (imposed on a strictly revenue-neutral basis, i.e., the proceeds of the tax being used to reduce personal and corporate taxes, and to pay for low-income tax credits to help offset the burden of higher fuel prices) would do no great harm, and we would gain from the experience an indication of what it might take to change behaviour sufficiently seriously to cut back on toxic emissions. This would imitate the process of social learning used in tobacco taxation to get people to give up smoking. These incentives would build on the heightened sensitivity to environmental concerns that have developed over time (and that should continue to be promoted), and that explain the successful impact on the behaviour of incentives to recycle, for instance.

For the time being, 'interventionist gimmickry' (as Martin Wolf calls it) like the so-called cap-and-trade regime

---

[40] How much should the present generation be asked to sacrifice to ensure that the standard of living of the population 100 years hence will not be 8.5 times ours but 9.5 times higher? Nigel Lawson, 2008, *op.cit.*, p. 93. The sooner this can be gauged, the sooner the charlatans will be silenced.

– a government-controlled administrative rationing system in which emissions are statutorily capped, and in which emitters are free to trade the permits which result from this system – would appear to be the flavour of the day. This sort of gimmick – pretending to be a market solution, that evolved from the Kyoto technocrats – is reminiscent of the sales of indulgences by the medieval church. The expert fixes are badly in need of replacement by more encompassing political responses.[41]

Conclusion

To borrow a phrase from one of Geoffrey Vickers' books,[42] this chapter "is concerned not with solving problems but with understanding situations." Problem solving is never more than 15 percent of governance; the rest requires a deeper understanding of less fully describable and less well-structured realities.

To deepen our understanding of the governance of sustainability, I have argued that what is needed is a new, open and creative approach; a new language; imaginative organizational design; and the construction of integrated beliefs and frames echoing the viewpoints of the different partners one wishes to influence. I have also argued that only polycentric governance (i.e., pluralistic regulated, self-governance) can deliver this outcome – one that does not allow the restrictive perspective of science to prevail in a trans-scientific world.

This requires a political blending of perspectives, so that decisions are not dominated by technocratic experts in the name of narrow scientific perspectives, even though the media propagandize it. The expert view has to be taken into account, but it is only one of many.

---

[41] This required politicization and escape from the tyranny of experts in the trans-science world reminds us of the apocryphal story about Georges Pompidou – reported by my colleague Richard French – who is purported to have said there are about three ways a public man might be spoiled and destroyed: women, gambling and listening to experts – the first way to perdition is the pleasantest, the second is the fastest, but the third is the most certain.

[42] Geoffrey Vickers, 1983, *op.cit.*, p. xxvii.

The next phase in the discussion should proceed beyond debates about whether there are self-governing structures that work – and there are – and focus on technologies of governance, about the definition of effective ways to get the job done. This is the work of social architects and social engineers.

As was demonstrated in some preliminary work we have recently done on this front,[43] this is likely to require a mix of incentive reward systems and of moral contracts.

---

[43] Gilles Paquet and Tim Ragan. 2012. *Through the Detox Prism: Exploring Organizational Failures and Design Responses.* Ottawa, ON: Invenire.

| Conclusion

" ... the word 'pneumopathological' to describe
those who are morally insane, 'living', as it were,
in a fantasy-world of self-righteousness ..."

Robert Sibley

n one of his essays, Robert Musil refers to *intelligent stupidity* not as an inability to understand, but as *a refusal to understand* – a disease of the mind based on a presumption of knowledge and insight that are not there, of orientation by emotion that overrules reason and creates blind spots, and of intelligence being used to invent convincing rationalizations for its ill-inspired viewpoints and actions.

The main purpose of the governance approach is to expose intelligent stupidity, and to challenge traditional paradigms, based on ill-grounded assumptions about the nature of governing in our complex and turbulent world, and on ill-inspired oversimplifications in strategy and policy. It questions the presumption of knowledge, the primitive and simplistic ways of defining problems, the arrogance, incompetence and disingenuity of pseudo leaders (who have only a portion of the power, resources and information), and the paucity of the work done to ensure the collaboration of all those who are necessary partners in any meaningful and effective process of wayfinding.

Chapter 3 sketched the contours of a social-learning *problematique* that proposed a more pragmatic approach not only to general governing problems but, in particular, to governing in the face of wicked policy problems. This approach modestly works hard at the description and investigation of the problem setting (instead of falsely presuming that these features are known), sets up exploratory inquiring systems, and focuses on the design of fruitful responses.

In Part II, this general approach is used to tackle the governance challenges created by concerns about equality, diversity and sustainability – problems where goals are unclear, and means-ends relationships are unstable or unknown. To bring the governance *problematique* to bear on these issue domains requires that various perspectives (economic, social, cultural, moral, etc.) be mobilized and blended if one is to generate adequate policy responses that are commensurate with the complexity of the problems.

Even though the issue domains explored proved to be quite different in tractability, some commonalities can be discerned in the ways in which the different wicked policy problems were examined in this volume.

Issues

The three problems discussed in Part II have in common that they all raise concerns expressed through *essentially contested concepts*. These concepts are defined by Gallie in terms of five conditions:

- they are appraisive, in the sense that they accredit some achievement;
- this achievement is complex in character, and its worth is attributed to the achievement as a whole;
- this achievement is variously describable in its parts with the possibility of various components being assigned more or less importance;
- it admits considerable modification in the light of circumstances; and
- each party recognizes that its own use of the concept is contested by other parties.[1]

---

[1] Walter B. Gallie. 1964. *Philosophy and the Historical Understanding.* London, UK: Chatto & Windus, p. 161.

Each of the three issues discussed in Part II meets these conditions. They are open to different perspectives and definitions; their content is multiplex; and, depending on what aspect is privileged, it can be appraised differently. As a result, reasonable persons may have very different evaluations depending on their perspectives. This plurality of reductive views entails that any one party only gains a partial view of the situation, and some blending of perspectives is necessary if one is to develop a less flawed, if still always incomplete, view on which to construct some effective wayfinding and governing apparatus.

The organizational texture surrounding and embodying these issues is polyphonic. It operates in many dimensions, is based on a number of separate and different points of view and codes, and speaks in many voices. However – contrary to the traditional polyphonic medieval choir, where each singer represents his own voice with a melody, text and rhythm of its own, but typically, is organized such that there is one singer in relation to whom the other singers conduct their voices – in the case of modern polyphonic organizations, *no such foundational organizing voice exists*. Getting the polyphony to emerge so that it will not be *cacophony* is the crucial challenge,[2] and this calls for multiple systems and codes (that are bound to endure) to be woven into somewhat coherent patterns.

These efforts are hard hit by pneumopathology.

Tribes having developed a focalization on one aspect or dimension of the issue (often to the total exclusion of others), as well as defence mechanisms to ensure that their particular point of view aggressively cannibalizes or at least dominates all the others, dedicate their intelligence and gumption to actively propagandizing it.

---

[2] Niels Åkerstrøm Andersen. 2003. "Polyphonic Organizations" in T. Bakken and T. Hernes (eds.). *Autopoietic Organization Theory*. Abstrakt Liber, Denmark: Copengagen Business School Press, p. 151-182.

Polyphonic organizations and hybrid forms of governance

Polyphonic organizations are not only pluralist in their fabric, but they are also faced with a great variety of voices in their environment. Thus, governing entails the dual job of attenuating variety and uncertainty somewhat, both internally and externally, with no hope of completely eliminating them.

This effort at coordinating and fostering collaboration is plagued by the cognitive dissonance, false consciousness and ideology of internal and external factions, so that getting a governing apparatus to emerge that is both as complex as required by the issue domain to be governed[3] and as effective as required to ensure resilience and innovation for the organization, is bound to be a daunting challenge.

In each of the issue domains explored in Part II, the primary challenge has been not to fall prey to cartooning the problem definition to such an extent that the very pluralism and idiosyncrasies of the core issues might be whisked away. For instance, assuming that someone is fully in charge, or that there is a framework or a set of functions that can be said to always dominate the scene, or that all potential partners share the same values and purposes: all this amounts to nothing less than assuming away the difficulties of governing in a polyphonic organization and context. In the three issue domains, nobody is fully in charge, no framework is hegemonic, and the potentially crucial partners or interested parties have different and often conflicting belief systems.

Moreover, in all three cases, the underlying social order evolves: it is quite different from one moment to the next, and is always somewhat fragile in our complex modern societies. Consequently, the governance process likely to be effective in generating meaningful wayfinding in a particular context is not likely to be available off-the-shelf. It has to be generated through exploration, experimentation and social learning. This sort of governance apparatus also has to cope with gaps

---

[3] Stafford Beer. 1974. *Designing Freedom*. Toronto, ON: CBC Publications.

between the imperatives of the terrain of realities as commonly observed, and the belief systems and presumptions invented by actors in the theater of representations.[4] On this road, nothing can be guaranteed, so the best that one can be expected to do is often nothing more than to provide a sketch of the contours of an inquiring system likely to work.

Coping with all these chasms requires hybrid forms of governance to reconcile the fractious interfaces; these hybrid forms can only generate ambiguities and paradoxes: "those involved in contracts want the contract to be more like a partnership based on trust, dialogue and community feelings; governing bodies of public expenditures want to have transparent and open profiles; the state wants to become a community; organizational decisions need to be flexible; fixing and not-fixing expectations at the same time. In all these cases, identities try to become exactly what they are not, and to be united with their constitutive 'other'. They want to unite with ideas or groups that they have previously had to exclude. The result is a hybrid form of governance."[5] These hybrid forms can only succeed in partially reconciling the different belief systems of the many parties into imprecise norms and rules with which they can live. The ensuing tensions do not necessarily generate clashes; most often they get resolved through accommodation that can only be partially successful.

Ambiguity and paradoxes abound in governance studies, and it is the very beauty of hybrids that they make paradoxes productive.[6] In all of the three issue domains that have been explored, polyphony has generated hybrid forms of governance, and the process of accommodation has entailed some suspension (or elision) of power by the party that is in a better position to exert pressure, in order to make the couplings or alliances work. But any suspension of power always entails

[4] Pierre-Frédéric Ténière-Buchot. 1999. *L'autre côté du miroir – Analyse structurelle et tablier des pouvoirs*. Paris, FR: Transition.

[5] Niels Åkerstrøm Andersen and Inger-Johanne Sand. 2012. *Hybrid Forms of Governance – Self-suspension of Power*. New York, NY: Palgrave Macmillan, p. 1.

[6] Gilles Paquet. 2012. "La gouvernance, science de l'imprécis," *Organisations & Territoires*, 21(3): 5-17.

the possibility of suspension of the suspension. Indeed, Niels Åkerstrøm Andersen suggest, hybrids are *imperfect deparadoxification machines*.[7]

Issue domains and wayfinding: mechanisms and representations

In each of the three cases, there has been a tendency for Big 'G' to prevail and to pursue strategies of centralization, coercion, and ideological brainwashing in dealing with wicked policy problems. We have suggested that, *a contrario*, the governance *problematique*, in the search for effective norms and mechanisms, tends rather to lean in the direction of decentralization, experimentation, and multilogue and accommodation, in the search for ways of reconciling the frames of reference and representations of the crucial partners. In fact, a bias for decentralization emerges naturally in governance studies, because it has generally proved impossible to tackle complex policy issues top-down. Both organizational texture and behaviours have to be modified, and action on both fronts requires adjusting to local and timely circumstances. Notions like the *carrying capacity* of organizations and institutions and the *discriminating altruism* that is called for in dealing with behaviour have been evoked as crucial constraints and major levers.[8]

Another bias in favour of experimentalism – and the use of prototypes and serious play with prototypes – has emerged in all files as one of the main features of the inquiring systems that are at the foundation of social learning. In a dynamic, pluralist, complex world, the challenge is not to discover a solution to a fixed problem, but to elicit and imagine a process capable of generating effective design responses to evolving situations. Given the inherent pluralism and the level of ignorance to start with, the only way out of this conundrum is to design a way

---

[7] Niels Åkerstrøm Andersen and Inger-Johanne Sand, 2012, *op.cit.*, p. 4.

[8] Both notions have been commented on explicitly by Garrett Hardin (*Living Within Limits*. Oxford, UK: Oxford University Press, 1993) in connection with the sustainability debate, and they cast an important shadow on the equality and diversity files.

out of the paradoxical situation through inquiring and social learning. The focus on the centrality of the design attitude and the learning loops in the governance approach brings the attention of the governance specialist to the continuous process of experimental reframing, restructuring and re-tooling, that, together with the construction of the requisite platforms of collaboration, holds the key to emerging strategies that can transform stalemates into non-zero-sum arrangements. This sort of thinking has permeated our three case studies.

A third common feature of the case studies has been the need to fight the constant attempts by one party or the other to impose a dominant frame, or a dogma, on the issue domain – a propensity that can only lead, if it succeeds (as it often does), to the collapse of collaboration, and ensuing dysfunctions and governance failures in the long run. When such dogmas acquire the seal of approval of the officials, the progressives and the media, and become part of the *pouvoir social*,[9] they become toxic mental prisons, and critical thinking becomes impossible. The road to accommodation is blocked.

In each of the three issue domains examined in Part II, such mental prisons have played a crucial role. Indeed, in each case, a certain freezing of the belief system has created a psycho-social and cultural stultification. While such blockages have often emerged organically, they have also been reinforced by explicit policy stances, and have become part of explicit *programming* crusades, that can legitimately be regarded as efforts to manufacture consent.

Two murky frontiers

Governance experts have systematically broadened their space and time horizons so as to be able to appreciate as fully as possible the ways in which the various dimensions of import impinge on the problem definition, and therefore on what might be regarded as an adequate response. This has allowed not only a better and thicker description of the issue domains, but also a more effective effort to ferret out the blockages (at

[9] Raymond Boudon. 2005. *Tocqueville aujourd'hui*. Paris, FR: Odile Jacob, 167ff.

the level of information, cognition, collaboration, organization, etc.) standing in the way of a promising direction to effective wayfinding. This has led to the smoking out of unwarranted assumptions, and also to opening minds to new and potentially promising directions for exploration.

This view from a elevating crane,[10] so to speak, has allowed us to expose the warts of egalitarianism, multiculturalism and deep ecology, and to elicit possibly promising general alternatives – equability, intermediate cosmopolitanism, and pluralistic regulated self-governance. This sort of improved description of the setting, and consequent detoxification, is only a first step in the unfolding of the applied governance *problematique*.

Imaginative institutional and organizational architecture and effective engineering of new sorts of designs – capable of resolving the paradoxes uncovered – need to follow. In this work, our various investigations have revealed two major sources of blockages that demand additional inquiry.

The problem of power

The mortgage of the Big 'G' (Government) cosmology of the past, and of efforts to cast the representations of the current world in terms of 'power over' is creating problems. Things have changed. Power has not disappeared, but has exploded and become diffused into various forms in the small 'g' (governance) world. It has transformed from power *over* by the one in charge, into a variety of arrangements of diverse sorts: power *with* (partnership), power *through* (manipulation), power *around* (coalition), power *between* (mediation), etc. So diffuse is the nature of power in modern societies that one might conclude, with Foucault, that power is everywhere.[11]

This leaves open the question of how power, in its diffuse form, should be taken into account in the governance approach. This has been done only in an *ad*

[10] Richard Normann. 2001. *Reframing Business*. Chichester, UK: Wiley, Part V.

[11] Paul Laurent and Gilles Paquet. 1998. *Épistémologie et économie de la relation – coordination et gouvernance distribuée*. Paris/Lyon, FR: Vrin, chapter 3; Gilles Paquet. 2012. "Le pouvoir est partout, " *Philo & Cie*, (1): 7-11.

hoc way through rough characterizations in the economic, political and social spheres, and with only limited success.[12] The governance approach needs to factor distributed power into its operations.

The most promising avenue would appear to be one inspired by the notion of the neural net: a set of nodes with a given level of activation, connected by communication links with different weights, depending on the strength of the connections between the neurons. In such a system, a neuron is activated when the signals that reach it are powerful enough and trigger a pattern of activity.

In a socio-technical system, the state of a network is a distributed pattern of power, corresponding to certain valences of the nodes, certain hierarchies of connections and certain coefficients of sensitivity of the neuron-like entities. Such a neural-like net is continually learning. As the network is activated, certain connections are strengthened, while others are weakened, which means that the pattern of power is modified, often in cascades. The neural net is said to 'learn': as constraints or new firings emerge, new alliances form, the distributed pattern of power evolves, and the structure of the organization is modified. The transversal distribution of power provides the network with the ligatures necessary for its unity and its capacity to learn.[13]

In this approach, the current state of the network is akin to the state of jurisprudence in the legal system. It represents a sort of automatic pilot, providing guidance at a certain moment, and activities all around contribute to an evolution of this jurisprudence collectively.

Until such time as a more satisfactory capacity to define and factor distributed power in organizations along these lines exists, the governance approach will be faced with a major obstacle in fully explaining the way in which such a

---

[12] For a review of the variety of ways in which power has been factored into organizational analysis, see Stewart R. Clegg et al. 2006. *Power and Organizations*. London, UK: Sage.

[13] This approach is further developed in Paul Laurent and Gilles Paquet, 1998, *op.cit.*, chapters 2-3.

pattern of distributed power affects the inquiring system and the process of social learning.

The opacity of the psycho-social-cultural-ethical pond

The second blockage is the relative opacity of the psycho-social-cultural-ethical world, in which the realities and representations that we have referred to are anchored. As became obvious in the case studies, to tweak the structures and the mechanisms meaningfully, one must take into account the world of representations, and delve into some quite elusive ingredients, like trust, honour, common public culture, fairness and the like, that are crucial components of the underpinning of the governance regime.

For instance, collaborative governance has to be able to count on *affectio societatis* – a true commitment of partners to engage in the *avventura commune* and to contribute to it to the fullest extent possible. Yet this elusive quality of the true partner cannot be presumed to materialize automatically, and it is not clear that we know much about the way to secure it. The same may be said about what Keats called *negative capability* – the capacity and will to keep going when things are going wrong. Yet these crucial elements are required if 21st century governance challenges are going to be met.

Some social scientists like Daniel Innerarity have developed a corpus of works probing the whole process of dispersion of power, and also the new socio-cultural-ethical opacity of our modern world.[14] But he is an exception. Yet without a better understanding of these underpinnings, there is little hope that we can really gain a meaningful appreciation of the forces that are shaping the dynamics of our governance regimes, and there is even less hope that we might ever gain a sensible appreciation of the ways in which power is evolving and being constantly redeployed in the world around us. Therefore, it is unlikely that we can generate the sort of general appreciation of these underpinnings that

---

[14] Daniel Innerarity. 2006. *La démocratie sans l'État – Essai sur le gouvernement des sociétés complexes.* Paris, FR: Climats; Daniel Innerarity. 2012. *La société invisible.* Quebec, QC: Presses de l'Université Laval.

is necessary to work usefully on the design of governing inquiring systems.

These are the new frontiers for social sciences.

In conclusion

In the complex patterns of connected relationships, no one is really in charge, and attribution of personal responsibility is often akin to whimsical scapegoating. But social scientists have not drawn the conclusions that necessarily follow from this observation. Indeed, the public debate continues to be overwhelmed by continuous efforts to develop pretentious constructs built on the assumption that someone is still in charge and on the determination to formally invent a guilty party even though there may not be one.

The only meaningful general response is a move back to chapter 1 and its section on the Quantum notion of governance, on the major principles that flow from it, and on the inquiring system that would seemed to be called for. Together with the exploration of the notion of distributed power, and the daring decision to trespass into the social-cultural-ethical world, these would appear to be the most significant blockages preventing governance studies to go forward.

Whether this quantum leap will be taken is not clear.

One may suspect that this might entail too many re-assuring certitudes having to be discarded for it to be done *de gaieté de coeur*.

For those who might find the pill too bitter, the challenge might be reformulated in the following and softer way: what is required from governance studies is nothing more than what Daniel Innerarity expects from philosophy: to bring a bit of subtlety and a taste for complexity to debates that have wallowed in puerile endeavours.[15]

---

[15] In the words of Daniel Innerarity, 2012, *op.cit.*, p. 10 "*... un petit peu de subtilité et de goût pour la complexité à des débats caractérisés par des reproches et des insultes à saveur infantile, à la marge des réactions automatiques d'un opportunisme médiatique qui évitent les thèmes compliqués et qui gonflent l'importance des lieux communs ...."*

References

Some segments of this book have been previously published or presented to public audiences in slightly different forms:

Chapter 1 was originally presented to the Institute of Public Administration of Canada Administrators' Colloquium, organized by Carleton University, at the Canada School of Public Service in Ottawa on March 27, 2012, and was subsequently published in a very different form in *www.optimumonline.ca*, 42(2): 99-121.

Chapter 2 was originally presented as a public lecture at the Telfer School of Management of the University of Ottawa on January 19, 2013, and subsequently published in a different form in *www.optimumonline.ca*, 43(1): 23-35.

Chapter 3 was originally published in *www.optimumonline.ca*, 43(3), at press.

Chapter 4 was published originally under a different title in *www.optimumonline.ca*, 43(2): 13-27.

Chapter 6 was originally delivered as the inaugural address to the First National Capital Colloquium on the Governance of Sustainable Development on January 24, 2004; a greatly modified version was presented at a colloquium of the sustainability program at Trent University in Peterborough on March 13, 2013.

Titles in the Collaborative Decentred Metagovernance Series

Other titles published by INVENIRE

www.ingramcontent.com/pod-product-compliance
Lightning Source LLC
Chambersburg PA
CBHW062054270326
41931CB00013B/3071